THE INTUITIVE APPROACH
TO READING AND
LEARNING DISABILITIES

THE INTUITIVE APPROACH
TO
READING AND LEARNING
DISABILITIES

A PRACTICAL ALTERNATIVE

By

DEAN F. HELD, Ph.D.

Assistant Professor
Coordinator of Education
Extended Degree Program
University of Wisconsin — Superior
Superior, Wisconsin

CHARLES C THOMAS • PUBLISHER
Springfield • Illinois • U.S.A.

Published and Distributed Throughout the World by

CHARLES C THOMAS • PUBLISHER

2600 South First Street

Springfield, Illinois 62717

© *1984 by* CHARLES C THOMAS • PUBLISHER

ISBN 0-398-04954-8

Library of Congress Catalog Card Number: 83-18059

Printed in the United States of America

SC-R-3

Library of Congress Cataloging in Publication Data

Held, Dean F.
  The intuitive approach to reading and learning disabilities.

  Bibliography: p.
  Includes index.
  1. Learning disabilities. 2. Reading disabilities.
3. Educational innovations. I. Title.
LC4704.H44   1984   371.9   83-18059
ISBN 0-398-04954-8

to my entire family
also to "Hans"
and all the wonderful
children like him

PREFACE

This book was written simply because there is a need for it. There is a need for an alternative learning-teaching approach, which recognizes the immense reserve capacities of the human brain and an expanded view of consciousness as it relates to learning and the learner as a whole person. It is dedicated to the countless number of intelligent, worthwhile children and adults who suffer the frustrations of not being able to learn by traditional methods and yet are forced to compete in that learning environment with devastating outcomes.

The Intuitive Approach is for anyone with learning problems. Whether it be a reading disability or learning disability matters not at all, since learning to read, or learning anything at all, is treated as an outcome of a quality experience and based on a number of important assumptions. It is well that the reader (teacher, specialist, school psychologist, and administrators) be briefly exposed to the basic assumptions prior to reading the text. These assumptions are supported by research as the various components of the intuitive approach are discussed throughout the text.

A. Children have great compensatory powers if freedom in the learning environment is provided.

B. If reading is treated holistically children will eventually develop their own personalized decoding system.

C. The periphery of psychosocial problems which surrounds the reading difficulty is greater than the reading act itself.

D. Thus the primary objectives of the Intuitive Approach are affective in nature, and learning to read is a secondary outcome.

E. The learning expectations of the student are a key factor and must be dealt with systematically in the clinical process.

F. The student must "start over" with a program that eliminates the learning barriers.

The intuitive approach is a philosophy, combining elements of humanistic psychology, suggestopaedia, cybernetics, language experience, psycholinguistics, wholebrain learning, and common sense. It is more than a philosophy, though, since a methodology has evolved and is being systematically researched. The key organization in the Western world is the Society for Accelerative Learning and Teaching (SALT) based at Iowa State University in Ames. The research center in Europe is at the University of Sophia, Bulgaria. Thus in this text, the words Suggestopaedia and SALT are used almost synonymously. The word "intuitive" is the author's own preference since this approach attempts to bypass logical, critical thinking and socio-suggested norms to provide an approach whereby severely "damaged" students learn to read automatically and economically in the human sense.

This text attempts to discuss the basic theory and rationale for an alternative approach to reading and learning disability and, more importantly, a method and procedure. The teacher's ability to be creative and innovative is the only limitation.

CONTENTS

THE INTUITIVE APPROACH
TO READING AND
LEARNING DISABILITIES

Chapter 1

A NEED FOR CHANGE

A RATIONALE FOR CHANGE

One has but to read Nila Smith's book *American Reading Instruction* and observe the fact that little has changed in the teaching of reading over the past few decades. The teaching method most commonly used yet today is the basal text approach. Historically, teaching practices have gone from individualized instruction to group-oriented (basal) instruction, and back to individualized. The most noticeable change is in content which changes periodically according to the socio-cultural forces in our society at any given time. We have, at least in some cases, moved from subject-content oriented emphasis to a sort of child centered focus. This renewed individualized orientation, I.G.E., or Individually Guided Education, has spread rapidly through the country but appears to wane at this time, even though certain traces of the movement will probably always remain.

The I.G.E. approach starts with the child, his needs and his interests, and moves him along at his own pace in whatever content the child needs at the time, in an approach that appears to have more flexibility and more built-in learning options. Thus, this movement does have its positive aspects but unfortunately there are as many brands of I.G.E. as there are schools doing it. The result of this is a hodge podge of educational practices that might be good for one child and devastating for another one. It is often negative in its orientation because it is frequently deficit centered with needs evolving out of countless hours of testing which further frustrate the human psyche. While this approach is a step in the right direction it still misses the true inner needs of the child.

Turning specifically to remedial reading, the diagnose-prescribe approach zeros in on deficits that are *results* of not learning and misses the *cause* of not learning. Too often all children are still expected to learn the same things in the same way and the only change is that pacing is differentiated. Schools that also focus on interest are one jump ahead of the others because, at least, they are beginning with the child's inner feelings.

Whether a school is traditional or progressive seems not to matter a great deal in comparison because educators have simply moved from a subject-centered approach to a child-centered one at a superficial level. The needs assessment is simply a measure of what skills a child has or has not learned and does not attempt to remove the cause of not learning. Good students have open minds and learn in spite of the teacher or method used. Research has not indicated that one approach is any better than the other since the key is the teacher with his or her understanding of how and why children learn and the child's "openness" to learn.

The purpose of this book is not to discuss methods for the child who is learning well but rather for the child whose mind is closed and who is not learning easily.

Since reading is still a primary mode of acquiring knowledge in our schools this skill will be a focal point but not the only emphasis in this book. Learning anything is secondary. It is an outcome of a quality experience, because true learning is automatic and appears essentially to be conscious and unconscious activity (62). The excellence of a child's oral language when he reaches school age is not related to excellence of "formal" teaching in his environment but rather to the "quality" of the interaction and communication that existed there. This example clearly illustrates that learning to talk was largely an unconscious outcome of that experience because it is the rich quality of the experience that keeps the mind open and produces a good self-image in the child. Petrie and Stone (75) indicate over and over again that one cannot be a good anything unless one can imagine oneself in that role.

There are available to the educator today some innovations that can help the teacher teach and help the child open up. But both must open up simultaneously. The programmed learning materials, audiovisual equipment and a host of other curricular inventions are not to be considered learning materials. They are tools and no more than bearers of content. The mind is the true learning material with a power that is unmeasurable if it is open and functioning. It is not possible at this time to measure true potential because, at the most, teachers can measure only what learning can be recalled at a certain time with what is being asked at that time. This is indeed a narrow measure.

If educators will open their minds and look beyond the content of the curriculum they will find answers that they never dreamed of before. You cannot pour water into a container without first opening the cover. This opening up is the "true readiness" for learning to read or learning anything at all. Teachers of beginning reading have always shown great concern for reading readiness, and rightly so, but the "true readiness" is ignored. Auditory discrimination, visual discrimination, right to left orientation and a host of other factors are emphasized. Again these are just tools to aid the decoding process and are meaningless unless the child is open to the reading act itself. One cannot and will not learn to read well until he can view himself as a potentially good reader. Blind people learn to read without visual discrimination and deaf people learn to read without auditory discrimination. Reading happens in the mind and not on paper. It is believing you can read and it is comprehending and appreciating what is read. The process an individual has to use to decode is less significant. Comprehension is not taught; it is developed in the open mind in conjunction with former experience and "here and now" attitudes about that experience.

The disadvantaged child, for instance, is said not to be able to learn to read easily because he lacks a rich background of experience and has a deficit in oral language development (105). Thus enrichment activities and oral language development are emphasized in the reading program. These practices appear to be sound and logical, but something is missing. Any teacher working in the ghetto or on an Indian reservation can tell you this by the number of failures that exist when the final product is observed. What then is missing? It is quite obvious that any child who has been programmed to fail before he enters school has to smell success before he can do anything but fail some more. Learning the initial consonants or the vowel sounds in isolation is hardly a prescription for success in the total reading act. Before a child can learn to read he must be open to reading, be a believer in himself and realize his potential first as a whole being and as a learner.

This is true in the case of any disabled reader regardless of his background.

> Jeff, a twelve-year-old disabled reader, came to the reading clinic for help at his mother's initiative. Tests indicated that he had problems with vowel sounds, word omissions, word substitutions, comprehension, etc., etc. Of course he did! Any poor reader will have these problems and it doesn't take a clinician and a whole battery of tests to find this out. He received the usual "drill on deficit" treatment without any effective results. It became very obvious that his self-image was at a low ebb. A new program ignoring reading directly was embarked upon. Two years later he was an honor role student with a new self-image. He saw himself as a learner and the rest happened.

How is this possible and what concrete methods are available to achieve this type of success? The answer is more simple than you as a parent or educator can imagine. The answer does not lie solely in colorful books and exciting adventures. That is the road; the vehicle is the mind that is fully functioning. Overhaul the vehicle first, and the drive down the road to success in reading will be easy.

The answers lie in the methods that are available to provide the "true readiness" for reading. For these answers we must look to a number of sources. The field of humanistic psychology and the works of researchers like Combs (26), Usher and Hanke (109) and others can provide the teacher with many insights. The work of Georgii Lozanov (62) in the field of suggestology is exciting and innovative. The related field of Suggestive-Accelerative Learning and Teaching with the work of Bancroft (7), Schuster, Bordon, and Gritton (93), Prichard (79), Held (38) and others is exciting and promising. Techniques in psycho-cybernetics (Maltz, 66) and hypno-cybernetics (Petrie and Stone, 75) will prove to be fruitful.

THE HUMANISTIC PRACTITIONER

Let us begin with the teacher and examine his role in educating our youth.

The improvement in the setting of conditions for teaching reading or any subject matter, appears to be the important task for educators today. Marcia M. Buchanan (18) indicated this when she wrote that "ultimately, our attempts to change are merely a manipulation of the internals, institutionally and socially accepted placebos, which seldom treat the illness and never seem to effect a cure."

The following statement by Fattu (32) supports Buchanan's contention also:

> It is commonplace but not very flattering to this commentator to deplore the fact that more than half a century of research effort has not yielded mean, measurable criteria around which the majority of the nation's educators can rally.

Since the Lozanov method emphasizes the teacher-pupil interaction on two planes, that is verbal and nonverbal, it is indicated that he is concerned with the internal aspect of feeling, personality, and attitudes that belong to the human psyche. If the study of external factors alone has not produced the key to what makes an effective teacher, perhaps researchers must look in another direction. Koff (55) who did an extensive review of teacher practices found personality development theory most seriously lacking in teacher training programs. He felt that teacher training institutions must consider in their programs the trainee's personality and the impact it has on teacher effectiveness.

Combs and others (26) have engaged in extensive research using counselors, teachers, and other professionals in an attempt to differentiate between effective and noneffective practitioners. Combs, Avila, and Purkey (27, pp. 12–16) concluded that this differentiation can be identified in their perceptual organization. People who are effective professionals:

> (1) Have internal rather than external frames of reference; (2) were more concerned with people than things; (3) were concerned with perceptual meanings rather than facts, e.g., more concerned with persons and reactions rather than material presented; (4) see others as capable, friendly, well-intentioned; (5) are not hampered by insecurities, doubt, and fears.

The above, supportive views, recapitulate Lozanov's Suggestopaedic Practice whose thesis lies in making learning a pleasant, rewarding experience through proper teacher-student interaction, by taking recognizance of both the verbal (external) and the nonverbal (internal) aspects of teaching. Thus, the human potential is more fully realized and the reserve capacity of the brain is stimulated by an induced or naturally produced learning environment.

It would appear, then, that the significance of this book lies not so much in the fact that it is a different approach, but in the fact that it is humanistic and tends to seek answers in another dimension.

On May 9, 1974, at the International Symposium on Suggestology, in Arlington, Virginia, Dr. Georgii Lozanov of the University of Sofia, Bulgaria, and founder of the suggestological approach, suggested that in many parts of the world, learning is a disease. We suggest to children, directly and indirectly, that learning is difficult and unpleasant. To paraphrase him further, he reported a great need to provide for students proper conditions for learning which are truly humanistic and are in themselves loaded with positive suggestions which lead to proper expectation of *all* the learners. This concept is certainly not new in our country but often appears to be overlooked.

According to Lozanov, expectation plays a key role in learning. The expectation is positive — "anyone can learn; learning is fun and is easy." This expectation belongs not only to the learner but also the instructor and the group as a whole. Nystrand and Cunningham (72) suggest that individuals are fully functioning when they are self-understanding, secure, sensitive, open to others, compassionate, searching, purposeful, enlightened, and responsible both to themselves and to others. They go on to say that fully functioning individuals become such by maximizing their own capabilities and aspirations through interchange with others.

The Maslow theory (67) holds that individuals must satisfy the lower level needs before higher needs even emerge. Since learning about the environment is stated as a higher need, Maslow's work appears to be supportive of the Lozanov method; whereby, proper conditions must be present to put students in the proper frame of mind prior to teaching the lesson content. Lozanov asserts that when a student is secure and relaxed the mind opens up if accompanied by proper expectation of himself, the teacher and others in the class. The Lozanov method makes use of techniques to facilitate or induce this in a calm suggestive learning atmosphere.

Usher and Hanke (109, pp. 2–10) also supported Lozanov's thinking quite directly when they listed the following basic principles that deal with man and his behavior:

(1) People behave according to their personal perceptions at the moment,
(2) the perception one has of himself is the most important and influen-

tial of all his perceptions relative to his behavior, and (3) man is continually engaged in the concrete search for self-actualization.

The aforementioned concepts are important to the Lozanov session in that students are put through exercises, both physical and mental, to provide for the relaxed, self-assured open mindedness needed to learn well. The Lozanov techniques, which will be discussed later, are used throughout the learning session to assure continuation of a relaxed and positive suggestive learning atmosphere.

This approach appears to be humanistic because of certain features that Lozanov discusses.

First, it is a direct method because it bypasses critical logical thinking and/or anxiety which a student might have. Second, the method is essentially automatic and effortless. Students are asked not to try too hard to learn (Schuster, Bordon and Gritton, 93). A third feature is its efficiency because of the directness and automation which is a result of lack of learning anxiety. The fourth feature is referred to by Lozanov as accuracy and is considered a direct result of the suggestion that learning is fast and easy. Economy is the fifth feature and points to lack of student fatigue upon completion of the suggestopaedic session; that is, the learning takes place in a completely relaxed, nonthreatening way.

Lozanov (61), Bancroft (7) and others stress the importance of proper teacher training to become an effective practitioner in the Lozanov method. The stress is put on the verbal qualities of instruction and student-teacher interaction as well as the nonverbal behavior of all involved.

Robert Blume (12), in his article, "Humanizing Teacher Education," summarizes so very well what is required of an effective teacher. This seems to parallel very closely the Lozanov ideology.

> The results of these (his) studies consistently indicated that effective helpers saw people from the inside rather than the outside. They were more sensitive to the feelings of students. They were more concerned with people than things. They saw behavior as caused by the here-and-now perceptions, rather than by historical events. They saw others and themselves as able, worthy and dependable; they saw their task as freeing rather than controlling, and as an involved, revealing, and encouraging process. (Blume, 12, p. 413)

At the International Symposium of Suggestology (May 9, 1975), Dr. Lozanov described what an effective teacher must be like. Combs (26) also described it similarly when he listed four qualities of effective teachers his research pointed to:

1. They tend to see themselves in essentially positive ways. That is to say, they see themselves as generally liked, wanted, successful, able persons of dignity, worth and intensity.
2. They perceive themselves and their world accurately and realistically. These people do not kid themselves. They are able to confront the world with openness and acceptance, seeing both themselves and external events with a minimum of distortion or defensiveness.
3. They have deep feelings of identification with other people. They feel *at one with* large numbers of persons of all kinds and varieties. This is not simply a surface manifestation of *liking people* or being a *hail-fellow-well-met* type of person. Identification is not a matter of polished social graces, but a feeling of oneness in the human condition.
4. They are well informed. Adequate people are not stupid. They have perceptual fields which are rich and varied, and available for use when needed. (Combs, 26, p. 70)

Combs (26) goes on to draw further research conclusions regarding effective teachers that recapitulate very well Lozanov's ideology regarding the role of the teacher in providing a healthy suggestive learning atmosphere.

1. Good teachers perceive their purpose in teaching as being one of freeing, rather than controlling students. That is to say, the teacher perceives the purpose of the helping task as one of freeing, assisting, releasing, facilitating, rather than as a matter of controlling, manipulating, coercing, blocking or inhibiting behavior.
2. Good teachers tend to be more concerned with larger rather than smaller issues. They tend to view events in a broad rather than a narrow perspective. They are concerned with the broad connotations of events, with larger, more extensive implications, rather than with the immediate and specific.
3. Good teachers are more likely to be self-revealing than self-concealing. They are willing to disclose self. They can treat their feelings and shortcomings as important and significant rather than hiding or covering them up. They seem willing to be themselves.
4. Good teachers tend to be personally involved rather than alienated. The teacher sees his appropriate role as one of commitment to the helping process, a willingness to enter into interaction, as opposed to being inert ... or remote from action.
5. Good teachers are concerned with further processes rather than achieving goals. They seem to see their appropriate role as one of encour-

aging and facilitating the process of search and discovery as opposed to promoting or working for a personal goal or a preconceived solution. (Combs, 26, p. 85)

Other characteristics of good teaching that Dr. Lozanov emphasizes are further supported by DeBruin (29, p. 243) when he concludes that

(1) good teachers are knowledgeable, (2) good teachers are sensitive to the individual student, (3) good teachers feel students are able and have the desire to learn, (4) good teachers are enthusiastic, no matter what technique or method of teaching is used.

Moustakas (69) describes a good learning session in terms of what a teacher must do: "He must reduce learner threats, enhance individuality, give learner respect and allow the learner to explore his own interests."

The Lozanov (61) method shows high concern for the affective domain and provides a sequence of techniques that will assure a comfortable and motivated affect, which, according to Lozanov, is essential to learning.

Fromm supports this contention when he spoke to the split between the intellect and the affect.

Anyone who wants to achieve must struggle against many basic trends of modern culture. One, the idea of *a split between intellect and affect*. This dogma of the split between affect and thought does not correspond to the reality of human existence, and is destructive to human growth. We cannot understand man fully nor achieve the aim of well-being unless we overcome the idea of this split, restore to man his unity, and recognize that the split between affect and thought, body and mind, is nothing but a product of our own thought and does not correspond to the reality of man. (Fromm, 34, p. 163)

To facilitate this change in the teaching process appears to demand a change in thinking among the many professionals in the teaching profession. While considerable research is available in humanistic psychology and its application to education, little is available to the reading practitioner about the Lozanov method regarding its efforts toward humanism and an effective way to operationalize it. The only known teacher's manual available in the Western world was written in Iowa by members of the SALT

Society (Society for Suggestive-Accelerative Learning and Teaching) (Schuster, Bordon and Gritton, 93).

Summary

Students fail to learn not because of lack of food but because of lack of appetite. The cognitive element cannot function without a healthy affect, and a reading teacher must find a way to reach the feelings and emotions within himself and the students. He must think in another dimension and help students to rise above the primitive blocks that exist in the unconscious. This is the "true readiness" for learning and the road to high expectation. This expectation cannot be reached until the student, the teacher, and the group as a whole is self-understanding, open, and secure within themselves and with each other.

Approach Used in Writing This Text

The Lozanov approach is now being adapted to remedial reading by only a few in the United States. The basic theory and methodology will be presented through an actual case study to provide for a better understanding of its application and strong and weak points. Actual lesson plans and theory will often be interspersed or, at times, presented in separate chapters. Later, you will meet a charming young boy with a deep-seated "Learning Phobia." This bright nine-year-old is batting zero in school and as a result is not batting much better in life itself.

Chapter 2

THE POWER OF SUGGESTION OVER LEARNING

SUGGESTION, HUMAN BEHAVIOR, AND LEARNING

Suggestology is simply the study of the science of suggestion, and cybernetics merely refers to the process of being steered by suggestion. There is nothing mystical or "far out" about this concept. It is not related to an occult, religion or some supernatural phenomenon. It is just a reality of how man operates in his environment as, by nature, he reacts in some way to all stimuli and each bit of information is stored in the unconscious (62). This accumulated series of reactions is the way man is programmed to behave in his environment. Reactions can be negative or they can be positive depending on the current situation and how the conscious and subconscious receives it in view of former experiences. If you hate shrimp, you react negatively when a stimulus makes you think of it; but if you like a certain food and smell it somewhere, you will react positively to the stimulus of suggestion and perhaps buy some or order it in a restaurant. Thus, your mind is either closed or open to the many suggestions that float around in our environment. Former experiences are stored in our subconscious mind and affect our behavior in all future events. Often man does not know why he hates certain things and is satisfied to continue to operate in a state of confusion. His mind remains closed and will not open unless he is taught to help himself or is retaught by someone else.

Thus suggestion as used here is not related to a "far out" phenomena but rather is the food of thought and the fuel for the engine of man's behavior. We can receive suggestions in many states of consciousness and the state we are in when we receive a stimulus often affects how we receive a stimulus.

If one is in a state of deep anxiety when company drops in

13

unexpectedly the reception will be cool in comparison to what the reception would be if one were in a calm relaxed state. This very calm relaxed state is often referred to as alpha (a calm state). If the anxious host has the power to come down to alpha quickly the reception will be more pleasant and remembered as a positive event.

In the same way that a person might react negatively to shrimp or to unexpected company a child might react to books, mathematics, or reading instruction. We do not necessarily have to alter the books, the shrimp, or the company unless, of course that is the cause of the negative reaction. Chances are that the learner or the host who is constantly in a negative frame of mind needs help. The reader can call this "help" whatever he chooses: suggestology, cybernetics, hypnocybernetics, reprogramming, or relearning; but it is just assistance in perceiving life situations or learning in a less anxious state.

If someone is sad, you help him by suggesting some activity that is fun or stimulating in a positive way. You are then reprogramming or helping him to alter his current state of being. In this process both the conscious and unconscious mind, of both involved, interact in ways that are not even understood by man at this time.

People in advertising are the real experts in the use of suggestion and its power. Just watch members of your family and their reactions to food or drink commercials. Even if you are turned off to shrimp a clever commercial using music, rhythm, color, intonation, and all kinds of gimmicks might be enough to reprogram you. There are strict federal controls on advertising because the power is there, and frequently the more indirect or unconscious the suggestion, the more powerful it is.

Any tool, even a shovel, can be a negative force if used wrongly. We cannot shun a tool because it is powerful. Then we would destroy something that is also beneficial to humanity.

As Lozanov (62) indicates, man is not a plaything in his environment. Man has a check and balance system that assists him in establishing a rapport with his environment. Lozanov calls this system anti-suggestive barriers.

Often educators have told a parent that his child is not learning due to a mental block. Almost as many times as it has been said, it has gone unexplained. The teacher did not know what the block was or what to do about it. The science of suggestology attempts to explain it and then do something about it by applying this knowledge to education.

ANTI-SUGGESTIVE BARRIERS

Lozanov (62) lists three barriers which he believes hinder suggestion or the ability of the individual to accept the content or even the instructor's suggestion that learning is easy and pleasant. The entire suggestological process is designed to break down these barriers and thus open the student to easy learning and raise expectations. It also provides for a direct information stream that bypasses logical-critical thinking and relies more on the archaic emotional and infantile mechanisms (Lozanov, 62). This method is, according to Lozanov, a suggestive-desuggestive phenomenon designed to desuggest the barriers to learning that are reportedly as follows: critical-logical thinking, intuitive-emotional barrier, and ethical-moral consideration.

Critical-logical Thinking

This barrier of critical-logical thinking is not making reference to critical thinking as discussed by Guilford in his Thinking Process Model (Klausmeier and Goodwin, 52). Nor does it appear that Lozanov is demeaning the important skill of evaluative thinking as described in Spache's model (Spache and Spache, 99). It refers, rather, to the personalized norm that is created in each individual as to how easy or how fast one can learn based on past experience. It has to do with the analysis of one's own ability to learn which has been suggested by former teachers or parents. Thus, according to Lozanov, the learning atmosphere must be filled with positive suggestion and a structure that will desuggest this personalized norm. Rosenberg (84) discusses the rigid-inhibited learner as having a strong need for structure and confidence and tends to adhere to preestablished value systems. This type of learner becomes disoriented when confronted with a complex situation and often withdraws. It is Lozanov's thesis that this type of critical-logical thinking about one's self must be desuggested. This problem is countered by suggesting that the child will be successful. It must be stated in an authoritative manner and the student must be assured that future results will prove it (Schuster, Bordon and Gritton, 93). Lozanov states that the teacher must also sincerely believe in his own suggestions.

Blitz (11) feels that some teachers may be so out of touch with their own feelings that they cannot tolerate feelings of others. It is thus possible, she goes on to say, that some teachers suppress students' feelings and interests in subject areas because they are not able to face their own feelings in those areas. Blitz suggests that teachers should not encourage the original feelings but find modes to help a child to overcome them. Lozanov presents his model as a possible mode.

Intuitive-emotional Barrier

Lozanov states that the intuitive barrier is more prevalent in children. The child will reject any suggestion that does not create confidence or security in the learning situation. Again, the learning atmosphere must directly or indirectly suggest confidence and security. The child must be assisted to reject the idea that he is unable to learn well. He must be put into a state that will help him listen and learn without reserves or fear. It must be stated and felt that learning will be easy and all will succeed in learning the content. Schuster, Bordon and Gritton (93) suggest that this must be stated firmly and without deception. Blitz (11) insists that the honesty and directness with which children are treated in the classroom enables them to use honesty and directness in their thinking and feeling.

Ethical Principles

The third anti-suggestive barrier has to do with the values and mores of a given society. The induced feelings that learning is unpleasant, hard work, and tedious must be overcome (Lozanov, 62).

Blitz cites educators who believe that children in our society have been conditioned to believe, because of existing conditions, that school and thus learning is full of boredom, hypocrisy, and hopelessness. School for many students is equated with confusion, hatred, and despair (Jackson, 44; Silberman, 96). Students exposed to or having this type of attitude toward school harbor feelings of insecurity in the school setting and lack confidence and expectation. The learning atmosphere must desuggest their feelings and attitudes. A direct suggestion to counter this barrier might proceed as follows:

> In the past many of you have felt that learning is hard work, drudgery and a bore. Here in this course you have to work but you will find that learning is easy for the effort you are putting in. You will learn very efficiently for that amount of effort. (Schuster, Bordon and Gritton, 93, p. 16)

The Lozanov suggestopaedic approach is designed specifically to come to terms with the anti-suggestive barriers of critical logical thinking, intuitive-emotional barriers, and ethical considerations. The essential components that authorities in this field indicate must be present in the learning situation will be discussed in the next chapter.

Summary

Man learns through his interaction with his environment by way of suggestive stimuli that saturate this environment. He processes these suggestions consciously and unconsciously in relation to former experience and often blocks out suggestions by way of the antisuggestive barriers which were described. This system of blocking is a necessary phenomenon since man would otherwise be bounced about aimlessly in his environment. However, there are times when individuals block positive suggestion that interferes with normal activity and the learning process.

An intuitive learning procedure based on the science of suggestion is a system that can eradicate those learning blocks and activate the full capacity of the brain to make learning to read or learning anything an enjoyable and successful endeavor. It is based on a number of related fields, such as: Psycho-cybernetics (66), hypno-cybernetics (75), suggestology and suggestopaedia (62), suggestive-accelerative learning, the language experience approach, and plain common sense.

Chapter 3

THE MAJOR COMPONENTS
OF THE SUGGESTOPAEDIC APPROACH

T he next three chapters will deal with the suggestopaedic components as proposed by Lozanov, which have been adapted to the intuitive approach (61). They will deal with the components of the suggestopaedic approach and facilitators of suggestion available for teachers in the learning environment. Later chapters will provide information about the self-steering techniques that will assist students in gaining a better understanding of themselves and enable them to set new positive goals for future success in learning. This process leads to the "true readiness" and provides the intrinsic desire and motivation to unleash the apparent and hidden potential within everyone.

The intuitive approach to learning, then, is based on suggestive theory and involves not only the teacher and his interaction with the learner but the student's ability toward self-steering. Table I will provide a schematic overview of the main components of this powerful method.

DEFINITION OF SUGGESTOLOGY

Suggestology is defined by Lozanov (61) as the science of suggestion through which we study the boundless world of psychic reactions which pass unnoticed and unconscious for the individual. Yotsukura (111) refers to suggestion merely as an important function of the human mind which plays a vital role in learning.

The purpose of suggestopaedia, according to Yotsukura, is to apply suggestology to pedagogy so as to create learning environments that will activate the reserve capacity of the brain. Or as Lozanov (62) states it, suggestion is the liberation from past suggestive complex and a new reprogramming by which the reserve

TABLE I
SCHEMATIC INTERPRETATION OF THE SUGGESTOPAEDIC APPROACH
(Author's Interpretation)
Developing a Suggestive Learning Environment

Facilitators of Suggestion*	Primary Mechanisms
Physical Relaxation	Authority
Mind Calming	Infantilization
New Names	Double Planeness
Music	
Psychodrama	Intonation
Imagery	
Self-Steering	
Confidence	Rhythm
Security	
Love	
Dramatic Presentation	Pseudopassivity

Expectation →	Open Mind →	Easy Learning and Memory

Anti-Suggestive Barriers are Overcome:
1. Critical Thinking
2. Ethical Considerations
3. Emotional-Intuitive

*Physical & Psychological Atmospheres are Suggestive.

areas of the mind are called to function. The reprogramming is often referred to as a nonspecific mental reactivity or the counter-action of anti-suggestive barriers and an establishment of a new suggestive set-up making reprogramming possible. Anti-suggestive barriers have already been discussed since they play a key role in the suggestopaedic practices.

Schuster, Bordon and Gritton (93) define suggestopaedia simply as a method that utilizes aspects of human suggestion and unusual styles of presentation to accelerate learning.

Lozanov cautions, however, that at this time one cannot say that suggestion is purely an unconscious activity. He states that it is impossible to separate the conscious and the unconscious since the information stream leading to the brain is cognitive, intuitive, emotional and subsensory. This information stream sets up conditions that affect motives, decisions and, in general, the conscious reserve of the brain and overcoming socio-suggestive norms that are already there.

Suggestopaedic practice then is a vehicle by which students are conditioned to react to positive suggestions in a learning situation so as to open the human potential and bypass current negative set-up regarding learning ease and efficiency.

MAJOR COMPONENTS OF THE SUGGESTOPAEDIC (INTUITIVE) APPROACH

The previous chapters discussed the intuitive approach in terms of humanism, since the suggestive learning atmosphere must permeate with security, self-confidence, and positive expectation about learning. The methodology which is designed to create this type of learning atmosphere and maintain it over long periods of time became known to the Western world through the works of Tashev and Natan (103) along with the work of writers Ostrander and Schroeder (73). It becomes evident in these works that the Lozanov method is not only designed to be economical in the human sense but to accelerate learning and improve memory. Lozanov of the University of Sofia, Bulgaria, has spent the past decade applying the science of suggestion to teaching practices in order to create conditions conducive to accelerated learning with improved retention. His work centered around changing the use of suggestion in a hypnotic state to the use of suggestion in the relaxed awake state (alpha). His work essentially involved two parts: the exhaustive study of the suggestive phenomena and the application of this phenomena to educational practice (Wolkowski, 110).

Lozanov proceeded to describe anti-suggestive barriers and ways to overcome these so as to make learning easy. This concept of creating a positive suggestive atmosphere and the process of breaking down learning barriers becomes the suggestive-desuggestive process Lozanov calls suggestopaedia.

This suggestive positive atmosphere is designed to make use of what Lozanov calls nonspecific mental reactivity which is the awakening of the reserve capacity of the brain and the reprogramming process. The specific purpose is to utilize a higher percentage of the brain power and reach out toward the person's total mental capacity (Schuster, Bordon and Gritton, 93).

Lozanov lists two complicated and four elementary mechanisms to utilize nonspecific mental reactivity in the suggestive learning atmosphere. These will be described, in order, as follows. It must be remembered that these components interact to achieve what

Lozanov calls hypermnesia, or heightened memory. While they can be defined, it is hard to separate them in actual practice since each component interacts so closely with the other (Lozanov, 61).

Authority

This element belongs to the instructor and refers to prestige and knowledgeability rather than the traditional meaning often assigned. It assures the instructor that the student will accept what he is saying as a suggestion and that the student will act upon it. It is an important factor in reaching the second component of infantilization (Schuster, Bordon and Gritton, 93). Lozanov considers authority important since it raises students' expectation levels and gives validity to content being taught.

DeBruin (29) also identified knowledgeability as an important characteristic of a good teacher and asserts that this factor affects how students view him.

When speaking about the authority component it is important to distinguish between authoritative and the authoritarian teacher. Katz (49) makes a distinction by calling the authoritarian a demanding teacher, while the authoritative teacher is strong, warm, encouraging, exact in explanation and demanding conformity when necessary.

Infantilization

Authority leads to the second important component in this approach, infantilization. Lozanov and others feel that during the teaching session, if students are in a childlike state (not childish), they are more open to learning suggestions; learning is accelerated and memory is improved. Thus, the right type of authority enhances the infantile feeling and along with other elements facilitates a pseudopassive state in which students listen and learn without reserve and without feelings of insecurity. This stage of infantilization might be likened to the openness and curiosity of the intuitive stage of learning Piaget talks about (Charles, 23). It appears to be the state that facilitates learning something without going through the analytic steps; that is: intuitive learning. Kneller (54) and Holt (40), insist that students learn more unconsciously than they do consciously and teachers repeatedly convince students they are unable to learn. This supports Lozanov's contention that there are socio-suggestive norms powerful enough to dictate one's reaction to suggestion and thus learning. These anti-suggestive barriers, such as critical thinking, must be overcome to provide a direct information stream to the brain. Other components follow that play lesser roles, yet important ones, in creating a positive suggestive learning atmosphere to open the reserve capacities of the brain.

Double Planeness

Double planeness merely refers to communication on two planes. The first plane is the verbal while the second plane is the nonverbal. Schuster, Bordon, and Gritton (93) pointed out that *how* an instructor says something is as important as *what* he says. Lozanov (61) suggests that the second plane, or the nonverbal level of communication, is very often underestimated or overlooked completely. It is important that both the verbal and the nonverbal are saying the same thing. The instructor must feel that the content he is teaching is important to him as well as to the student. He must show this by enthusiasm in his voice as well as in his expression and gesture. Yotsukura (111) supports Lozanov's theory that each mental activity has central and peripheral parts. The center bears the semantic content upon which the learner acts, but the learner also reacts to the entire complexity of the mental activity. The latter is indicative of the second plane activity or nonverbal communication, such as gestures, gait, mimics, eye movement, and facial expression. The second plane, then, is an enormous signaling system radiated from a person unconsciously or not sufficiently conscious. It has been indicated by Lozanov (62) that the two planes must be harmonized in the learning setting. Peter Kline's work as reported in *The Washington Post* (104) reflects the same thinking in his efforts to integrate the body, mind, emotion, and spirit into the learning process. There is further support concerning the power of the second plane.

Church (24) speaks at length about the concept of behavior mobilization and the contagiousness of moods, emotions and atmospheres which belong to many group situations and probably the classroom. Lowen (50, p. 15) spoke about the second plane when he said:

The character of the individual as it is manifested in his typical pattern of behavior is also portrayed on the somatic level by the form and movement of the body.

Intonation

Another primary mechanism in the approach is intonation. This is often, according to Lozanov (62), an element of double planeness in that various intonations indirectly suggest authority, mood, and attitude and can create an atmosphere of expectation. With every intonation there is a release of unconscious mental power since it is considered an expression of internal feeling. Students also seem to prefer it because it delimits boredom and is more pleasant. Thus, in content presentation, material is given not only in a natural voice but also in loud authoritarian voice as well as in whispered tones. This dynamic presentation with creative variation helps keep the students' attention over a longer period of time (Schuster, Bordon and Gritton, 93).

It is well known in the reading field that intonation helps students grasp full meaning and feeling when learning new words. Burron and Claybaugh (19) imply that intonation gives the content being presented an artistic or emotional tone. Trauger (107) said that a listener responds first to intonation signals rather than to words; he also responds to rhythm, stress patterns, and tones of people around him before he responds to the words. According to Pettinger (76), spoken language is very complex and subtle with much being communicated by intonation. The before-mentioned supports Lozanov's thesis that intonation is vital to the suggestive learning atmosphere since it helps set the emotional tone, facilitates double planeness and provides for expectation.

Rhythm

Lozanov considers rhythm a basic biological principle of our everyday life such as the annual seasonal changes and of day and night itself. Rhythm is widespread in the arts and advertising and has in itself suggestive value.

Rhythm, when combined with intonation, provides for ease of learning and memorization as when a child learns a song (Lozanov, 61).

In the Lozanov approach, the instructor often presents his material with rhythm after synchronizing it with the student's breathing or background music (Schuster, Bordon and Gritton, 93). This further enhances the suggestive relaxed atmosphere, increases attention and opens the mind to learning. It seems apparent that intonation and rhythm are used extensively to awaken the senses in such areas as advertising, song and drama. As Siks (95, p. 152) explained:

> Everything in life has rhythm—a graceful swallow, a swiftly darting king salmon and a willow tree. Every child is a rhythmic being, each with his own unique rhythm and pace. A child's rhythm begins with the beat of his heart which sends the surge of life through his entire being. He breathes, eats, sleeps, walks, thinks, feels and talks in rhythmic patterns.

Siks goes on to say that rhythmic movement is a child's natural way of expression and thus becomes a natural way to learn. It appears that all good primary teachers have made this discovery and the suggestological method uses the rhythmic tool to provide more effective teaching for people of all ages.

The poet Langston Hughes (42) said, "Deep inside of men and animals there are rhythms we cannot explain, but they are part of life."

Pseudopassivity

Research seems to show that a passive mind enhances suggestion and its effects on learning (Schuster, Bordon and Gritton, 93). It has been shown that when students are in a calm state their learning capacity is substantially increased (Lozanov, 62).

The aforementioned components appear to be a unified concept with one component supporting, facilitating, or even being an outcome of the other. According to Lozanov (62), the authority component facilitates infantilization which in turn has the outcome of the pseudopassive component. Pseudopassivity, ease of learning, and volume of material learned are also aided by intonation, rhythm, and double planeness. The students' level of expectation in the learning session is also created by the proper utilization of the basic complicated and elementary components just mentioned.

Lozanov (62), Bancroft (7) and Schuster, Bordon, and Gritton, (93) and others provide support that the complicated and elementary components can create a suggestive positive learning atmosphere which in turn provides for desuggestion of former negative attitudes about learning and fears of failure. It opens the mind to a fuller capacity to learn. It results, according to Lozanov, in hypermnesia, or heightened memory, with an activation of the reserve capacity of the brain. Specific data which apparently supports this heightened ability to learn appears in Chapter 14.

Extensive use of this approach has been applied to the teaching of foreign languages. At this time one has to turn to the work of Held (38) and Prichard and Taylor (79) to find evidence of its value in the remediation of learning problems.

It has been implied so far that the primary emphasis is to create a suggestive learning atmosphere. There appears, however, to be another emphasis, which is to learn as much material as fast as possible. As mentioned, most of Lozanov's work has been with the teaching of foreign languages. Bancroft (7) states that the reported learning of 1800 new words or word groups per class session (3–4 hours) is an extravagant rumor spread by some commercial organizations in the United States. The actual norm that she cites is 80–100 new words or word groups and corresponding grammar per day.

Accordingly, the claim that language training has been speeded up by a factor of fifty to one is probably an exaggeration, also. The United States research, according to Schuster, Bordon, and Gritton (93), indicates that learning has been speeded by a factor of three to one.

Summary

The aforementioned components are important elements in the intuitive approach, since authority, infantilization, double planeness, and pseudopassivity must be present in all sessions. The use of rhythm and intonation vary greatly according to the situation and will be discussed in later chapters where specific directions are given as to classroom implementation of this suggestological or intuitive approach.

Chapter 4

THE INTUITIVE TEACHING SESSION— A SUGGESTOPAEDIC MODEL

In the previous chapters, the major components and facilitators of the suggestological approach were presented individually in definition and an attempt was made to discuss the approach in terms of what has already been recognized in American educational practice by some educators. It appears that some components of this methodology have already been recognized by many educators, but emphasis on certain components is often lacking. It appears that an emphasis on maintenance of a positive suggestive learning atmosphere over time is not always achieved. A conscious effort to desuggest reduced learning potential in the students has also been absent along with efforts to maintain learning expectancy. As mentioned earlier, the components are so interrelated that it appears difficult to separate them in practice. This chapter will discuss one way the methodology is practiced and how the components can be applied along with suggested adaptations.

At the International Symposium of Suggestology (May 9–10, 1974) in Arlington, Virginia, Dr. Gabriel Racle disclosed to the author the sequence and organization of the suggestological session. Table II will schematically illustrate this sequence. This particular organization as presented, is used for teaching Spanish or French to English speaking students, college age or older. Racle studied with Lozanov and is Director of the Suggestopaedia Program for the Canadian Public Service-Staff Development Branch in Ottawa, Ontario.

This model will serve as background for the reader so as to make later adaptations easier to understand. While it appears necessary that the teaching session has specific divisions and time allotments, there is considerable flexibility in structuring the teaching sessions.

26

Table II

THE SUGGESTOPAEDIC SESSION

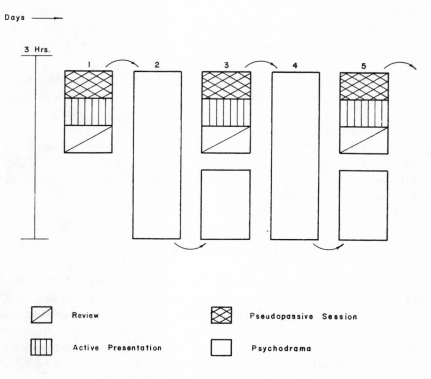

◨	Review	⊠ Pseudopassive Session
▥	Active Presentation	▢ Psychodrama

THE REVIEW SESSION

The daily language sessions usually run from three to four hours with short breaks between sessions. The review portion is a rather traditional review of the former day's material, which lasts about thirty minutes each day (Racle, 81).

However, according to Schuster, Bordon, and Gritton (93) it might also include the acting out of dialogues through use of skits and paired conversation. Usually the printed material is directly in front of the learner during this review session. The particular objective of the review session is to summarize the previous lesson and give added opportunity for reinforcement. It is important that the student be properly prepared prior to this beginning session. Physical exercise and mind calming activities such as discussed earlier are participated in to properly assure a relaxed state and an openness to suggestion. These suggestions are positive and the student is assured that learning will take place and his inhibitions toward learning have been overcome. It might be suggested that they will learn with the openness of the mind of a child. This was referred to earlier as infantilization; or, it might be suggested that this learning experience will be as pleasant as an earlier learning experience they have been asked to recall (E.P.L.R.).

The levels of expectations must originate from the instructor and student to be maintained by the instructor's behavior both at the verbal and the nonverbal levels. Lozanov (61) refers to this as double planeness as was discussed previously.

Bancroft (7) states that beginning with this review session, the student is encouraged by a positive yet authoritative instructor. He is given a new name and a new role to play at the beginning of the course to further reduce learning inhibition and is encouraged to accept this role during all sessions.

THE ACTIVE SESSION

It is during the active session that the new language material is presented, both visually and auditorily, usually in the form of dialogues. The content begins with familiar things the student sees about him. Material is arranged in triads which facilitate intonation and rhythm. The first phrase is given in a whispered tone, the second is natural and the third phrase in a loud voice. Furthermore, the three phrases are presented in exact rhythm (Bancroft, 7). According to Lozanov (61), this whispered tone imitates the experiments his staff is carrying on with subliminal suggestion.

Schuster, Bordon, and Gritton (93) stress the importance of utilizing the dramatic and dynamic style of teaching. They feel that parrotlike repetition is noninspiring and the learning process should be an enthusiastic, creative process. The emotion is more important than the exercise. Joyce (47) and Torrance (106) support this contention. The varied rhythm and intonations used in the Lozanov method, then, are vehicles for this dynamic creative presentation of materials during the active session.

Bancroft (6) discusses the importance of the outward concentration toward the printed text being presented as well as the inner repetition of the words or phrases being taught. Inner speech is considered to be of prime importance in Soviet psycholinguistics.

The triad organization of material has value beyond that of facilitating a rhythm. Enough time must be allowed within the triad for words to be thought about and repeated in whispered tones. It is further suggested that students be trained to make use of vivid imagery and word association techniques to aid the learning and retention of the new material being present (Schuster, Bordon, and Gritton, 93).

Research at Iowa State University (Schuster, 88) suggests that words that are sensorily experienced with all modalities are more easily learned and retained. That is, students are asked to experience the material as fully as possible, to hear, see, feel, and taste the words. Day and Beach in research reported by the International Reading Association (43) also support the multi-modal approach.

Bancroft (7) states that the rhythm most commonly used for presented materials during the active session is 2:4:2. That is, two seconds are used to state a phrase in the known language. Then the phrase is repeated in the foreign language being taught in the next four seconds. Then there is a two-second pause. Thus, there is a time span of eight seconds per reading of the known language phrase and the foreign translation for each of a triad of three phrases. Twenty-four seconds would then be used for one triad. This rhythm is maintained throughout the presentation during the active session. Schuster, Bordon and Gritton (93) recommend that the instructor vary the rhythm only as the occasion dictates. They reserve the exact rhythmic pattern for the next session which is called the pseudopassive session or passive concertlike phase.

THE PSEUDOPASSIVE SESSION

Yotsukura (111) likens concertlike pseudopassivity to the unrestrained perception of the environment as that of a child. This student is in a state similar to one attending a concert and listening to music. In a classroom, the students relax, breathe deeply and listen to music while the instructors act out or read lesson dialogues with intonation and deep feeling. According to Yotsukura, Mozart music seems to be most appropriate.

Schuster, Bordon and Gritton (93) describe this pseudopassive state of mind as being relaxed and full of stimulation and expectancy. While Bancroft (7) suggests dynamic presentation during the pseudopassive session, Schuster recommends that the instructor speak in a normal authoritative tone of voice. But in accordance with the Lozanov recommendations, both of these authorities use the same 2:4:2 rhythmic pattern as during the active session. However, during this passive session, the rhythmic presentation of content is synchronized with breathing and music. Thus, the student inhales for two seconds. An example for teaching a Spanish word would be as follows: "Breathe in (1–2) mesa (*may*-sah) — table — mesa (1–4), breathe out (1–2)."

At the same time, the instructor orchestrates his delivery to the rhythm of the music. Bancroft (7), Schuster, Bordon, and Gritton (93) recommend baroque music. In any case, music selected should have about sixty beats per minute. Music, then, seems to serve several purposes during this passive session. It provides a relaxed concertlike atmosphere, facilitates the rhythmic presentation and as Bancroft states, "Liberates the mind from earthly concerns." Students are requested to use the same imagery and sensory feeling as during the active session.

THE PSYCHODRAMATIC SESSION

This session is allowed the largest time block and has as its purpose reinforcement and practice of dialogues learned during the active and passive sessions. It consists of plays, skits, paired discussions, learning games and the like. The dialogues are practiced in a realistic way by acting out true life situations. Students may actually go out to cooperating stores, restaurants, hotels or to other appropriate establishments to practice and get firsthand experience in practicing the language.

The Lozanov/Racle style of suggestological practices in education has been very effective for foreign language training. (See Chapter 3.) Dr. Jane Bancroft (6, p. 13) who visited the University of Sofia, Bulgaria, to observe the Lozanov method summarized the approach as follows in the *Canadian Modern Language Review* (March, 1972).

> While the class generally follows a ritualistic pattern in which the new material is "reinforced" three times, once the students have achieved a

certain command of the foreign language, they go "into the street" to practice it. They must be able to describe their environment in the foreign tongue. Since the language material is presented to them in dialogue form, students are also asked to present simple plays in class. Although the classrooms in the institute are small, an area in front is set aside for the acting out of plays.

Dr. Lozanov and his colleagues have found that their system speeds up the assimilation of a foreign language and that, because of the "relaxation" session, course members feel little or no fatigue after a four-hour class. Vocabulary and grammar are "absorbed" without the intense effort normally required for memorization. Students are able to converse easily. (I conducted part of an English class in which the students could carry on a good, if elementary, conversation after five days classwork.) They are also apparently able to recall their verbal knowledge on tests administered up to a year after a given session.

Whether language classes in Bulgaria are "traditional" or "experimental" in nature, their success can be attributed in large measure to the motivation of the students and the training and enthusiasm of the teachers. Instructors put in long hours; students are obliged to attend every class. The authoritarian atmosphere does not appear, however, to dampen the teaching process. Indeed, according to language teachers of various "schools" authority, when used in a positive manner, increases the expectancy of the students and furthers their learning of the foreign language.

The suggestopaedic approach as proposed by Lozanov stresses the use of relaxation and suggestion in the aforementioned structure. This author proposes certain adaptations for working with younger children who have learning problems. The Lozanov style approach puts great emphasis on teacher-directed suggestion and does not emphasize training in self-steering or self-reprogramming for young children. Thus, the intuitive approach involves both the teacher directed and self-directed activity in educational practices as future chapters denote.

ADAPTATIONS

The three and one-half to four-hour sessions for college level training in foreign languages seems to work well. However, in a remedial session, with students who are "tuned out," this time allocation would be burdensome. Younger children, with their shorter attention spans, would need shorter sessions with appropriate breaks at one hour intervals. Students normally have about a six and one-half hour school day with frequent changes in pace built into the schedule. Activities such as recess, physical education and nonacademic subject matter provide the needed change of pace.

In a remedial session for reading disability students the following adaptations might be chosen according to the needs of the session. The rationale for each model becomes apparent in the discussion that follows.

Table III

THE TEACHING SESSION

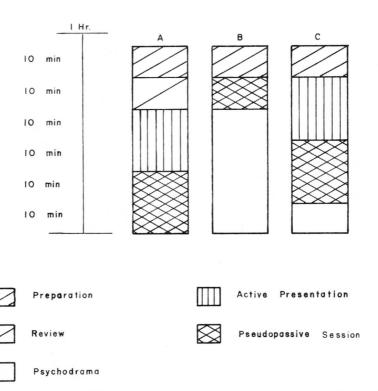

The preparation period is a must for each session regardless of what is to follow. This is when the student is either assisted to relax, become alert, self-assured, and open to learning, or is capable of this self-induced state. Directions similar to what have been discussed earlier will be used. This involves physical and mental relaxation techniques. The exercises mentioned are only suggestions and the teacher need only use his imagination to come up with others. Students should use deep vivid imagery during this portion of the session. Children will very easily write their own imaginary trips which can then become material for their own vocabulary development. Perhaps a trip in a flying saucer or on a hot air balloon could be used.

If a review session is necessary, it can follow in a rather traditional manner. If the preparation period is effective and repeated often enough, the relaxed, or alpha, state will be maintained throughout the review and active session to follow.

During the active session, new vocabulary and meanings or other content are presented and discussed. The content, or new vocabulary, is usually an outcome of a language experience that involves imagery and positive suggestion. This will be discussed in great detail later.

The content is again repeated during the pseudopassive session. Students are asked to listen passively and relax to music. Intonation and rhythm provide for a creative delivery.

The above described session followed sequence "A" Table III. The sequence that follows will depend on the needs at that time which are dictated by students needs, follow-up activities desired, or reinforcement needs. Perhaps sequence "B" would be necessary. The required relaxation session takes place again. Perhaps a review of material by way of the pseudopassive method would be appropriate. If the material presented was of great volume perhaps a psychodramatic session is in order for further reinforcement: a skit, a role playing session, learning game, or creative writing. Perhaps sequence "C" could have been chosen as well.

Thus there are five basic segments that the intuitive learning session is composed of. These are ordered and sequenced according to the needs of the time. Any experienced teacher can make the judgments as to this sequencing.

Table IV will simplify the entire concept and might be preferred by some teachers.

Table IV reduces the session segments to a simple three-segment concept. All three are required to properly implement the intuitive approach. From this viewpoint psychodrama, presentation, and review are simply lumped together under one roof. The nature of any given active session will again depend on the needs at a given time.

TABLE IV
SIMPLIFIED SESSION

	Activity	*Time*
Preparation	a. Teacher directed relaxation period b. and/or student self-steering	Minimum 10 minutes "Depends on students' needs"
Active Participation	a. *Presentation* of material by teacher b. and/or *use of psychodrama* games, interaction activities, choral reading, etc. for general reinforcement c. vehicle for simple *review*	Decided by needs at the time
Passive Participation	a. students listen passively as content is repeated. *Note:* Rhythm and intonation work well in this session. Authority and double planeness enhance intuitive learning.	Depends on volume and difficulty of content

NOTE: The review session also works well prior to the preparation phase.

Generally speaking, sequence is not as important as the ability of the practitioner to provide a quality experience full of expectation and positive orientation for the learner. The greater the ability of the teacher to divert the learner and make the content an integrated part of the experience, the greater will be the results.

Summary

The intuitive learning session has five basic segments: preparation, review, active session, pseudopassive session, and psychodramatic session. These can be reduced very simply to preparation, active participation, and passive participation with each segment having the obvious objectives as stated below.

A. To prepare the students for the learning session.
B. To provide for multi-modal active participation in the learning experience.
C. To provide for passive reinforcement of new content learned and create an intuitive learning process.

Chapter 5

THE PREPARATION PHASE—
"AFFECTIVE VERSUS DEFICIT TEACHING"

RATIONALE FOR AVOIDING DEFICIT TEACHING

If a child with reading problems is to be helped it will not evolve out of his measured deficits alone, since the deficit is a result of not learning, and placing the immediate emphasis there will not remove the cause of the problem. If a child does not know his vowel sounds it "might" hinder somewhat the decoding process. If the cause of this particular deficit is due merely to the fact that the vowel sounds were never taught to him before, then teaching the vowel sounds in this case is an appropriate action. It is doubtful, however, in the case of a middle grader that he has never been taught vowel sounds. If the child can hear and see discriminately in a consistent manner, it is then a matter of a possible mental block about reading that must first be removed. How a child sees a letter is not important as long as he discriminates consistently and is consistent in assigning sounds to symbols as he sees them. Experts in the reading field provide long lists of deficits that the disabled reader can have and the usual corrective procedure is to use any number of tests to find the deficits and then prescribe activities accordingly. It is well known that most children have had the word recognition skills taught to them over and over again as they progress through the grades. Even in the most progressive schools today, teachers fail to ask themselves this question: Why didn't Peter grasp certain decoding skills the first time they were taught, or the second, or the third? Instead of asking this most important question, elaborate testing and charting devices are used to list every deficit "Peter" has. Often deficits are advertised by plastering charts all over the classrooms. Then not only does Peter worry about what he does not know but so does everyone else from the janitor to Peter's tennis partner. Thus the problem is magnified and Peter becomes even more certain that he will never learn to read. To confound the problem even more Peter has always been in a low group ("Blackbird") and has been programmed to respond accordingly. His own personalized expectation has been set and he behaves and achieves in that relationship. To assume that Peter will learn all of the skills needed to decode simply by putting him through a crash phonics program is foolhardy. First his learning expectation must be changed so he is able to imagine himself being a good reader and really believe it so that the reteaching will be much easier.

In the first place he has probably succumbed to one or more of the anti-suggestive barriers as described by Lozanov (62). Thus his initial training must be desuggestive in nature coupled with positive suggestion and immediate success.

IMPROVING THE LEARNING ATMOSPHERE

The true story of Jim who had always been a "Blackbird" and had the whole list of problems associated with poor readers is a good example. The teacher inadvertently gave Jim an "A" in reading when Jim was accustomed to getting "D's" in reading on every report card. Well Jim was thrilled and it seems the whole family celebrated over that "A." The teacher didn't have the heart to tell the truth and thus let it go through. Fortunately the teacher recognized Jim's improvement the next quarter and gave him another "A." The deficits suddenly began to disappear. This one incident was enough to desuggest Jim's inhibitions regarding reading and provide positive imagery about himself as a reader. The positive reinforcement of this new "imagery" by the teacher helped Jim maintain his new expectations.

Teachers should not wait for an accident to change a student's image of himself in a learning situation. Jim was able to cancel out his former expectation in his subconscious mind and once this cancellation took place his reprogramming began.

Not all cases are as easily remedied as Jim's proved to be. But techniques are available to the teacher, school counselor, and reading specialists to reprogram students attitudes and desuggest the learning problem. Yet teachers, counselors, and even school psychologists are not being trained to do this. Professionals are trained to be content and deficit oriented and have been programmed to teach in a certain way. This does not happen only because of teacher training programs but it happens because "teachers have a tendency to teach the way they were taught."

As mentioned earlier fields, such as psychocybernetics (66), hypno-cybernetics (75), and suggestology (62), have powerful applications in the field of education. These fields coupled with the much-used language experience approach and with creative activity provide a new and exciting outlook. The methods will be viewed as productive and commonsense approaches once they are experienced. Teachers must experience them first before they can teach children to benefit from them.

The outstanding works of Petrie and Stone (75) along with the research of Maltz (66) will provide the teacher with some enrichment aids. By combining these techniques with previously discussed classroom teaching strategies a new dimension in the remediation of reading problems is born.

Students, parents, administrators, and all supportive staff in the school community must first be made aware that the techniques are sound practices and not dangerous brainwashing tools. They are not deep-trance hypnotic episodes. The techniques are used to develop relaxed states of consciousness to put the conscious and subconscious in a state of rapport. Once this is achieved the student can and will be able to desuggest his own inhibitions, and establish new attitudes and learning expectations. The procedures are simple and nonthreatening to students, as will be illustrated here.

PREPARATION FOR THE ACTIVE AND PASSIVE PHASES

Petrie and Stone (75) have a simple, but powerful three-step approach teachers can use to teach students how to help themselves through "self-steering." They are similar to the following steps:

1. Teach the students how to achieve a relaxed state.
2. Establish conscious-subconscious rapport.
3. The students use vivid imagery and self-suggestion or teacher suggestion to change their attitudes about learning.

Step 1. Relaxation

Have the students sit relaxed in a comfortable chair with their feet flat on the floor. Then follow any of the relaxation techniques as suggested in Chapter 3. Deep breathing, whereby a student simply attends to his breathing, might in most cases suffice. However when students are particularly tense it might be necessary to use some of the muscular relaxation techniques as suggested in previous chapters. The students' hands should be lying relaxed on the thighs. Once complete relaxation is achieved the student is ready for the next step.*

Step 2. Establishing Conscious-Subconscious Rapport

Once the child is relaxed vivid imagery is used to help the child desuggest his inhibitions and to relax even more. The child should engage himself in the white cloud exercise as mentioned earlier and pretend he is being pulled up into the cloud. Once he gets the feeling of being pulled up into the cloud he is ready for step three.

The reading clinician or teacher will have to direct this activity at first, but eventually the child can do it by himself. Other types of deep mental relaxation exercises similar to the white cloud exercise can be used. Another exercise children enjoy is to pretend they are watching a large hot air balloon float high into the beautiful sky. They pretend they are being pulled up with it. Once they get the feeling they are being pulled up by the gentle power of the balloon they are ready for the next step. They must be free of worry and fear at the moment of suggestion that follows.

Step 3.

The child is now very open to suggestion about his status in relation to learning and ease of achieving. He can set new goals for himself for all his future endeavors not only in relation to learning ease but in relation to his own self-image. The sugges-

---

*In a recent experiment conducted by the author, students' reactions to relaxation techniques were so favorable that parents noticed them doing these exercises of their own accord at home. This experiment involved sixty-four fifth and sixth graders. Their reactions were totally positive as evidenced by remarks such as: "I feel so good in that class" or "That class is so much fun I feel so relaxed and happy." Chapter 14 discusses this experiment in greater detail.

tions should at first come from the teacher, but later the child should pick up on these and participate in self-suggestion, or as it is more appropriately called, when working with children, self-steering.

Here the teacher might use Early Pleasant Learning Recall which was discussed in Chapter 4 and will be repeated here.

> Try, with these directions to imagine and visualize to the best of your ability. Now return to an early pleasant learning experience where you were eager to learn and before you had your memory skills impaired. Pick an early school experience or one where a parent was reading an interesting and educational story (pause). Get the details of this early pleasant learning experience as fully as possible in your mind. Use your imagination as necessary to fill in the following information. Feel yourself back in the situation and room again (pause). What people were around you (pause), what was the name of the teacher or parent (pause), recall how your hands felt in this situation (pause), what thoughts were you thinking (pause), how did your throat and head feel (pause), what was your feeling (pause), what was your emotion (pause). Get all of these details very clearly in your mind (pause), hang onto that eagerness, and learn this lesson the same way. (Schuster, Bordon and Gritton, 93, p. 31)

As will be seen in a later chapter, E.P.L.R. has been used quite successfully in the teaching-learning setting. It appears to be a powerful tool.

There are many other suggestions the teacher should make while the child is in this relaxed state of rapport.

What is suggested by the teacher has tremendous impact on the students. It is of great importance that the teacher be in a state of mind that is conducive to establishing and creating a good learning atmosphere. Children are very perceptive to both the verbal and nonverbal behavior of the teacher, reading specialist, or whoever is conducting the class. As Rosenthal and Jacobson (85) state: "The teacher's tone of voice, facial expression, touch and posture may be the means by which—probably, quite unwittingly—she communicates her expectations to pupils."

The practitioner must really believe what he is suggesting because the child will surely perceive his true feeling either at the verbal or nonverbal level. He must help the child to set new goals and expectations in a way that there is no doubt but that this will in fact happen. The nature of the teacher's suggestions will depend on what the needs of the student or students he is working with are. The following are some possibilities and notice their positive orientation:

A. This lesson will be fun and easy for all of you. (E.P.L.R.)
B. You will always learn easily and find it rewarding.
C. You are just as good as anyone in your class and can learn as easily as the rest.
D. Books are fun to read.
E. Don't worry about words you don't know, they come to you easily.
F. You can do anything you want to do if you really believe you can do it.
G. You are just as capable as that person you are thinking about.*
H. You are a happy, bright person and will now believe it.

The process that you are working with is attitude formation or perhaps more correctly called attitude reformation. In a recent publication by the International Reading Association, Alexander and Filler (1) made the following conclusions about the importance of self-concept and attitudes toward reading that seem to summarize the rationale for this approach.

1. *Past experiences.* A low self-concept may be caused by the child's poor evaluation of his reading performance or by the evaluations of those individuals whom he likes, such as parents, peers, and/or teachers.
2. *Counteractions.* A learner who feels that he may not be successful in the eyes of individuals important to him may attempt to avoid the reading act. He may use such avoidance behaviors as disinterest in or hatred of reading, apparent lack of effort, or refusal to read.
3. *Self-concept reinforcement.* The learner may reinforce his own self-concept. If he believes he will not succeed in reading because of some previous experience, he actually may not succeed.
4. *Spiraling process.* Because of his self-concept, the reader may become progressively better or poorer with reading. Success generally leads to greater effort; failure tends to cause less effort, which results in progressively poorer performance as the learner advances in school. (Alexander and Filler, 1, pp. 6–7)

It is important to note that not only are self-image and attitude toward reading important factors in learning to read, but recent research by Alexander and Filler (1) concludes that attitude to-

---

*All children have heroes or heroines they follow closely. A good technique is to have the child (while in Step 3) vividly imagine himself being like that hero. The teacher then follows with the suggestion stated in "G" above.

ward the content of what is being read is important and can affect comprehension of it. This has considerable implication not only for the reading specialist or clinician but the regular classroom teacher. The use of mind opening devices and techniques to change reading attitudes is of little value unless followed by activities that provide success and create a proper learning atmosphere. The work of Kemper (1) suggests some specific things a teacher should keep in mind when teaching children to read or when teaching anything. These suggestions apply to the intuitive approach in every sense.

1. Being aware of children's attitudes toward certain aspects of reading, thereby planning reading activities toward which students are more favorably inclined.
2. Using reading materials in which students can succeed.
3. Using materials related to the interests and needs of the student's norm group.
4. Providing situations where the usefulness of reading is apparent, such as requiring certain reading for completion or for participation in an interesting project.
5. Demonstrating a personal value of reading by practicing it orally or silently so that students can observe the teacher's high regard for the activity.
6. Providing for recreational reading.
7. Using reading material found in the student's everyday world.
8. Encouraging parents to improve their child's attitude toward reading by reading to him, providing him with reading materials, and setting an example by becoming a reading parent.
9. Avoiding the use of reading as punishment.
10. Using bibliotherapy, i.e., guiding children to read books in which they encounter problems and people relating to their own worlds.
11. Being very enthusiastic when teaching reading.
12. Being positive in the teaching approach—emphasizing existing abilities rather than frequently referring to the errors and inadequacies of the child. (Alexander and Filler, 1, p. 10)

The above are important thoughts and must be considered carefully since they are "feeling" oriented and far more important than approaching reading through a reading skill-deficit orientation. Skill deficit reteaching should be an incidental thing which goes on unnoticed by the child. This is very contrary to the diagnose-prescribe approach being advocated today. This writer would add two more important concepts to Kemper's list:

1. The teacher must present himself in a prestigious manner.
2. The teacher must provide stimulating activities whereby learning is an automatic outcome of that event.

Recent research by Lozanov (63) indicates that students learn and remember easier and in greater volume when they view the instructor as an understanding yet authoritative person, because it gives the content credibility. Furthermore, when a learner achieves infantilization, or is in a childlike state of consciousness, learning becomes an automatic outcome of a good quality experience.

Summary

The preparation phase is crucial since it is here that the "coming down" begins and a relaxed secure atmosphere is created leading to elevated levels of suggestibility. It is generally teacher directed in the clinical setting, but children should be taught to practice it on their own as well, since it will make the preparation phase more effective.

The teacher must always keep the primary objectives of the preparation phase in mind:*

  A. To create a relaxed and secure learning environment free of the suggestions that reinforce the student(s) learning inhibitions.

  B. To create conditions of hypersuggestibility and provide for positive suggestion and self-image improvement.

  C. To provide the content for the active phase which follows.

---

*The teacher usually uses a physical exercise followed by mind calming activity such as white cloud. Mind calming activity usually leads to a fantasy trip which becomes the content for a language experience story during the active phase. This provides for an integration of what happens in the preparation phase to what eventually transpires in both the active and passive phases.

Chapter 6

THE ACTIVE PHASE:
INTUITIVE LEARNING ACTIVITY

The previous chapter contained suggestions regarding the preparation phase of an enrichment session using the intuitive approach. This first phase might be of ten or fifteen minutes duration at first but with practice and training can be reduced to approximately five minutes. Since mild calming, opening up, and development of a state of hypersuggestibility are the primary objectives of that phase, transition into the active phase is of prime importance.

The active phase involves multi-modal activity, while the preparation stage is mainly visualization or imagery with self-suggestion or auditory suggestive input by another party. The transition is to be gentle and involves an activity that closely integrates what was done in the preparation stage. While the active phase does demand student involvement using all sensory channels, the altered relaxed state achieved during preparation must nevertheless be maintained. This chapter will provide the reader with a model to follow that will assure this maintenance.

Of primary concern is the severely disabled reader who is so turned off to reading that the mention of that word triggers an automatic turn off. Consequently the primary objective of each lesson is centered on building self-concept, mild calming, and attitude change. The secondary objective is the automatic learning of new reading skills. Thus the activity must be high powered, emotionally positive and bear the content in total disguise.

Let us use the following as an example lesson which integrates the preparation phase with the active phase in smooth transition.

LESSON EXAMPLES

Lesson Example One

Preparation Phase:

Objective—To develop pleasant and positive feelings about learning.

    A. Relaxation

    B. Establish rapport between conscious-unconscious feeling about learning. Read the E.P.L.R. instructions to the individual or group and suggest deeper relaxation.

    C. Have student visually and sensorily relive that Early Pleasant Learning Experience. Suggest that what you experience next will be just as much fun.

Active Phase:

Objective—A social experience in sharing that precious moment.

Teacher: "I could tell by the smile(s) on your face(s) that you have a wonderful experience. Let me tell about a wonderful experience I had learning how to. . . . " (The teacher must have a good experience ready to share.)

Teacher: "Let's share our exciting learning experience with each other." Children who are going to work together should be encouraged to share. However do not force it, because usually the shy child comes forth when he sees the teacher's enthusiasm and upon hearing about all the experiences others in the class have had. The teacher continues to emphasize the quality of the *experience* not the quality of the oral presentation of the child.

Teacher: "Those were exciting moments and they are important to you and should be recorded for future enjoyment in your Experience Journal."*

Teacher: "I'm so anxious to see your story written down and will be happy to help you if you need me."

---

*If the child (or children) is not willing or able to express his experience in writing the teacher will do it on chart paper or on the chalkboard. In the case of a severely retarded reader the teacher will do all of the writing.

While the students are writing the teacher must circulate and give help where needed but always praise the experience. At this point success must be measured by the quality of the experience and not by the quality of the writing. The writing and sharing is secondary to the experience but is nevertheless the vehicle of remediation. The written product should be very brief and written on any scrap paper the first time.

When everyone has finished writing his experience the teacher takes the next step cautiously.

Teacher: "While you visit with each other I'm going to read about your experiences and then give them back to you so you can record them in your journal." (This immediate feedback is essential.)

The teacher must not pretend that the writing is free of error. The child already knows he has made errors and will appreciate *you* making the corrections before returning the paper. When handing the paper back to the child make a positive remark about the *experience* which will relate personally to each child. The child will then rewrite the story into his Experience Journal and whatever corrections he makes in doing so will be incidental to the experience itself.

Once the experiences are rewritten children are encouraged to share and read to each other orally, or if they prefer they can read about each other's experiences silently. *Never* force oral reading. The teacher should always read orally with the child.

The teacher, using a chalkboard or flash cards reviews key words and problem words that she perceived so as to provide an overview of the experience as well as to provide the visual and auditory stimuli related to content, vocabulary, and word recognition skills. Students should mentally visualize the words and their structural parts, but attention is not called to phonic elements since children will discover them.

Other activities of a psychodramatic orientation can follow the writing and sharing. These activities raise the spirit and put life and activity into the active session. There are many ways to share experiences.

1. Pantomime.
2. Pairing off to write and perform skits.
3. Role playing.

4. Puppets should be available for the child to use. (Preferably made by the student.)
5. Making up and singing songs centered around this experience.*
6. Remember that old-fashioned whole word drill is essential, but handled in a different way.

The passive session will be discussed in the next chapter in greater detail. Here it will suffice to say that the teacher, within the active session, is collecting material for her presentation during the latter part of the active session and the passive session. The passive session must be a spontaneous and a powerful reinforcement of the active session. The teacher must either jot down or make mental notes of words and skills the group has trouble with. These words and skills will be presented auditorily to the class by the teacher as she relives the experience. This will become clear in the next chapter, and the teacher will soon see that this is a powerful way to teach problem learners.

To make the procedure used during the active session clearer to the teacher another example will follow. Remember that the basic principles are relaxation and mind calming to produce hypersuggestibility, teacher or student self-steering through suggestion, conscious-subconscious rapport, quality experiences, and intuitive learning as a natural outcome. The primary objective always centers around a quality experience, which provides positive attitude building and bears at the same time the content to be learned.

Lesson Example Two

Preparation Phase:

Objective — To be whoever you want to be.

A. Relaxation — suggest that students relax (Step 1).
B. Establish rapport between conscious and unconscious.

Teacher: "Decide who you want to be. It can be anyone, just anyone. Visualize in your mind how this person looks,

---

*The teacher must be creative and dramatic and lead the way by her performance.
It is of great importance to remember that the *experience* is the primary vehicle and the language arts skills learned are secondary, because they should be an automatic, intuitive outcome of that experience.

how he acts, how great he is—you are now becoming him and you feel different somehow—you feel good and can do anything you want to" (Step 2).

Teacher: "Imagine now the things you can do now. Imagine whatever you wish. What can you do now? How do you look doing it? Great!"

The teacher must also engage in this activity to prepare herself for the sharing and to allow time for the students to use and develop vivid imagery.

Active Phase:

Objective—See the new me. I can do what I want.

A. You all look so confident and happy. I'm feeling that way too. Let me tell you who I am and what I can do.

B. The activity that follows each imagery can be varied greatly according to the mood at the time. The teacher must become mood oriented and spontaneous in activity selection. If the group has loosened up they might pair off to write a skit which is immediately performed. The teacher must be highly enthused and participate fully by leading the way and doing the activity along with the students no matter what this activity happens to be.

The students should write a brief description of "Who Am I" for today's journal entry. The emphasis remains on the experience and the hero worship aspect. This is a powerful tool when coupled with imagery and writing. The teacher should make ten to twelve flash cards to review, with the students, words they mispelled. These will also be used during the passive session.

The teacher must be alert to conceptual aspects of the activity and again jot down notes so she gains further insight into the technical aspects of the child's reading and writing problems. She must grasp the mood and the vocabulary that carries this mood so that vocabulary and word attack skills can be approached incidentally during the passive session.

This structured intuitive approach is obviously for students who have severe reading problems and deep-seated self-concept deficiencies. Students who are less retarded in reading will benefit from this approach as well, even though their self-concepts have not been as severely damaged. Good readers and learners will be greatly enriched by the imagery experiences for promoting the stimulus for book selection and creative writing topics.

When students begin to trust the teacher and begin to view reading as a desirable activity, transition to books can begin. Do not rush this or push for early transition, because the mental readiness for books might take time in coming. As you engage in imagery activity of various kinds a pattern of interests will become apparent for each child. As these interests become apparent, the teacher should begin to saturate the environment with books but not force their use, even though they might be appropriate at the moment.

Summary and Lesson Illustration

Children who are turned off to reading are often so threatened by reading activities that they consciously or subconsciously tune it out. Crash phonics programs are not the answer since they do not get at the root of the problem. The problem often lies in overall self-concept, or one's image about himself in the reading act, or even a confusion about what reading really is. These feelings and negative attitudes must be desuggested so a pleasant outlook can be developed in relation to the reading act. At the onset of clinical help and continuing until a change of attitude is achieved the teacher needs some concrete tools to work with. Children who are fearful and anxious attend to those feelings first and thus turn off or can not handle the content being taught. The purpose then, of the preparation portion of the lesson is to relax the mind and body through suggestion and imagery and create a new or altered state of consciousness so learning suggestion can be received.

The activities severely disabled readers should engage in during the active phase must at first be integrated closely to the imagery used during the preparation phase. This focal point is attitude centered and remains the primary focus of the lesson. The activity also provides a secondary aspect, learning to read and write better even though it is never mentioned. This may seem overprotective to the reader but it is not since the teacher is attempting to break through the child's self-protective shield. As the child becomes less protective the teacher can become more direct. But until that happens the reading improvement must be an automatic-intuitive outcome of the experience provided.

The procedural progression to this point is as follows: Relaxation → mind calming → altered states of consciousness — suggestion → attitude-centered learning activity and indirect learning. In time it should evolve into: Improved self image → improved attitude toward reading → raised levels of learning expectation → appreciation and *easy reading.*

Following chapters will present many more lesson ideas to provide a more intuitive learning approach.

Summary — Lesson Illustration — Preparation and Active Phases

Preparation Phase:

    A. Relaxation (teacher suggested).

    B. Establish conscious-unconscious rapport (use a breathing exercise, and/or an imagery exercise).

    C. Continue imagery exercise (i.e., take a white cloud imagery trip with teacher suggestions that contain positive learning feelings).

Active Phase*

Suggested activities:

    A. Share orally an imagery experience.

    B. Write about the imagery experience. (Together or individually depending on the students.)

    C. Using word flash cards, have students see the key and problem words, say the words and with eyes closed vividly imagine seeing the words.

    D. Act out the experience.

Passive Phase:

See Chapter 7.

---

*Old stories are usually reviewed daily as the last activity in the active phase, even though it is seldom mentioned in the lesson plans.

Chapter 7

THE PASSIVE SESSION

OBJECTIVES

This session is often called the pseudopassive session (61) and infers that the student is relaxed and listening passively with an open mind. The objectives are as follows:

A. To maintain the new learning expectation and altered state of consciousness.
B. To reinforce positive feelings about learning.
C. To reinforce the importance of the experience.
D. To reinforce the content learned in the active session.
E. To stimulate imagery.

While this passive presentation is totally relaxed it is also a time to engage in more reinforcement of vocabulary or other skills. Ambiguity and subtlety are maintained by inducing other stimuli.

The rationale for the passive session can be explained easily by citing Burron and Claybaugh (19) when they suggested that a child responds to the nonverbal aspects of reading before he does to the verbal parts. This is an important concept and is employed in the passive session by providing a creative presentation using background music, intonation, and rhythm. The students listen passively while the teacher voices new vocabulary or spells words with meaning attached or with the use of context clues.

Bancroft (6) suggests use of baroque type music because it is soothing and lifts the spirit. Younger children might enjoy music that is modern and more appealing to them and this is fine as long as it is soothing and enhances passivity. Teachers should choose whatever music seems appropriate for the age-group but play it softly so as not to distract the student entirely.

The reader will recall that in the previous chapter lesson examples were given for the preparation and active phases. This is just a beginning of the tremendous creative experience that can evolve out this approach. In example Lesson One, an imagery experience called E.P.L.R. (Early Pleasant Learning Recall) was used as a relaxation technique and later integrated into the active phase by sharing and writing. The teacher, as it was suggested, must either jot down or take mental notes about what the students are writing and the words with which they are having problems. She must also grasp the key words that carry the emotion and set the mood, because the teacher must feel this mood and express it during her presentation. Varied rhythm and voice intonation are the tools at her disposal. Let us use the E.P.L.R. lesson as an example and carry it through completely. The preparation is the usual three-step procedure, but the procedures will vary somewhat. The variance often lies in steps two and three. At times they are integrated and at other times they need not be depending on the overall lesson plan. The reader should take notice of this with this lesson example and those to follow so as to discover the various possibilities.

OUTLINE OF LESSON EXAMPLES

Lesson Example One

Preparation Phase:

Step 1   Relaxation—the teacher has the students engaged in muscle and breathing exercises.

Step 2   The teacher reads the E.P.L.R. instructions to the students to establish a conscious-unconscious state of rapport.

Step 3   Deeper relaxation is achieved through use of imagery. The students are asked to relive as sensorily as possible this early learning experience. The teacher makes positive learning suggestions.*

Active Phase:

The students share their experiences orally and then write about them. The teacher immediately corrects the papers and returns them to the students for rewriting in the Experience

---

*Steps two and three are, in this case, integrated.

Journal. The teacher then proceeds with the lesson through use of flash cards using words which are key words and problem words. The students receive both auditory and visual stimulus and respond by orally spelling out the words, acting out words, or practicing the words in pairs. (The teacher may use an activity that is nonthreatening and lots of fun. Imagery, or mental visualization of the words, is also a good idea.)

The following pages will go into detail on how to carry the lesson through to completion by engaging in the passive session.

Passive Phase:

The teacher has grasped the mood, key words, and problem words as the content for this presentation.

Teacher:	"I'm going to turn on some music while you relax and I relive with you parts of your experiences."

The teacher will change voice intonation and expression as suggested in the following example.

Teacher:	"John had a wonderful experience when his Dad taught him how to ride a horse."
(N.V.) Normal Voice:	"John got on the horse."
(Wh.) Whisper:	"Horse—"H-O-R-S-E"
(L.) Loud:	"The horse jumped."
N.V.:	"Jumped—"J-U-M-P-E-D"
Wh.:	"John hung on tightly."
L.:	"Tightly—"T-I-G-H-T-L-Y"
N.V.:	"John never fell off."
Wh.:	"Joan had fun learning to cast for fish."
L.:	"Cast—C-A-S-T"
N.V.:	"Fish—F-I-S-H"
Wh.:	Etc.*

In this way the teacher relives the experiences all the students had while spelling key words and teaching phonics with intona-

---

*Words and their spelling can be repeated several times at each intonation level.

tion and rhythm only: Note that the words spelled are key words and words that might or might not have been misspelled. The phonetic elements are also included here and are added vehicles of rhythm. For example the spelling of fish—beat 1—f, beat 2—i, beat 3—sh said together quickly so as not to orally separate consonant blends and digraphs. (Beat 4—pause.) The same was true for the word cast. ("c—a—st"—pause). A different intonation can be used for each sound.

The teacher must use body language and facial expression to help carry the mood and retain the nonverbal quality of the lesson. This is crucial in the intuitive learning process. While a triad (three levels of intonation) is used, rhythm can vary from triad to triad or level to level. Schuster, Bordon, and Gritton (92) have found that keeping in time with music enhances learning and provides for another interesting dimension. If the music is in four-four time, the teacher might try to follow this beat.

This approach is catchy and appeals to children of all ages just as seen in Sesame Street® and television commercials. Children learn commercials and catchy songs without trying, thus giving us an example of automatic intuitive learning. The intuitive approach imitates the creative rhythmic quality of the learning modes that children in this society prefer and have grown up with.

It must be noted that the auditory stimulus is the essential one in the passive session. Since one wishes to maintain passivity it is best not to saturate the experience with direct visual stimuli. Should the teacher wish to use visual stimuli, such as pictures or flash cards, this whole experience could then happen in the active session instead of the passive one. Visuals appear to cut down on mental imagery development which is an element the teacher wants to evoke during this session. With eyes closed, students are asked to visualize the words and their parts.

This is an opportunity for the teacher to be creative and spontaneous along with the opportunity to use the child's own experiences to correct attitudes about reading and resulting deficits. It will require a shift in thinking on the part of the teacher and a loosening up to provide a free, open learning atmosphere. The experienced teacher will have already recognized that the essential components of this approach are not new. The use of music, language experience, and drama are not new to American educators. This lesson sequence as it is presented makes the approach more tangible and manageable. It adds the elements of imagery, relaxation, and suggestion. To be effective using the intuitive learning process requires some practice and a realization that the teacher is free to improvise. The three-phase sequence seems to be important, but in terms of time allocation and creative activity it is limited only to the teacher's imagination.

For the sake of clarity another example is being provided now. "Let your imagination run wild as you experience it. Ask yourself, how would I change it; how would I enjoy it? What would I do to improve it?"

Another Intuitive Lesson

Objectives: To develop ease of learning.
To develop imagery.

To develop new vocabulary (jungle animals).
To develop the recognition of the "f" sound in ph and gh and other sounds as they appear.

Preparation Phase:

Teacher: "Everyone relax now. For a few minutes let's attend to our breathing. When you breathe in, think in. When you
Step 1 breathe out, think out. Don't think about anything else. Just relax." (You too, teacher).

Teacher: "Today we are taking a trip in a hot air balloon, so close your eyes, relax and enjoy the trip. What color is the large balloon? What color is the gondola? You are stepping inside. How does it look?" (Pause) "What do you find inside?" (Pause) "What did you take along for the trip?" (Pause) "You are beginning to rise. Feel yourself
Step 2 rise high into the sky—feel it." (Pause) "Look down, what do you see?" (Pause) "Look up and see the beautiful sky." (The teacher can expand in vivid language making Step 2 a joyful experience.

Teacher: "You are now floating in the sky—what a wonderful trip

you will have. Look, we are over a jungle. See the ele-
phant with his large trunk. Look at the lion with her
cubs. See the bright birds." (The teacher would prepare
carefully in advance so as to describe vividly what is
Step 3   seen.) Then the teacher is silent to allow students to see
things on their own. "What do you see? Take it in and
enjoy it. It's fun to learn this way."

Active Phase*

Teacher: "Wow, what a trip. Let's talk about everything you saw."
(This should be a free sharing period. If a child saw a
farm cow in the jungle, accept this with good humor.)
Some possible activities:

A. With the help of the students write a brief story on
the chalkboard or on chart paper incorporating
everyone's ideas.

B. Have students write their own stories or copy the
group story.

C. Act out or pantomime animals' actions letting students guess what it is. As they guess write the word
on the chalkboard.

D. Have a rhyming word game:
Child One: "I saw a tree."
Child Two: "I saw a bee."
Child Three: "I saw a big cat."
Child Four: "I saw his hat." (Etc.) (A fun way to work
on word families.)

Passive Phase:

The teacher puts on the music softly while children relax. The
teacher now knows what John saw and what Jane and the others
saw on the trip in the hot air balloon.

The nature of the teacher's dialogue in the passive session is
dictated by the children's experience in the active stage.

---

*The experience continues to be the focal point. The language development is merely an
outcome. There is no accountability because there are no tests! But the experience should be
recorded in the student's journal for future enjoyment. (Again, phonic elements are induced
only incidentally since the basic assumption of this approach is to allow the freedom a child
needs to develop a personalized decoding system.)

Teacher:

(N.V.) Normal Voice:	"I saw an elephant—E-L-E-PH-ANT."
Wh.) Whisper:	"And thats not enough—E-N-O-U-GH."
(L.) Loud:	"E-N-OU-GH"
N.V.:	"John saw a fat cat."
Wh.:	"Fat—F-A-T" (Pause)
N.V.:	"Jane saw a tree and a bee."
Wh.:	"Tree—TR-E-E"
L.:	"Bee—B-E-E" (Pause)
N.V.:	Etc.

The dialogue is spontaneous and has come from the children's response. Remember they have already had visual exposure during the active phase.

Summary

This passive auditory presentation is merely reinforcement stressing key words, trouble words, and phonic elements. The children will learn easily if you believe they will and stress creative experience. Keep in mind that it might take time and patience to allow the children to open up and believe they can learn painlessly.

The possibilities are endless and as infinite as the teacher's imagination. The sequence as presented along with the suggested components have been tested empirically and appear to be of value. (See Chapter 14.) Within this framework great freedom can be exercised by the creative teacher.

The lesson examples thus far have suggested a close integration between all phases in terms of content and theme. Once students open up and trust the teacher and their own ability to learn this integration is not as crucial. Thus the preparation phase can occasionally incorporate a relaxation exercise such as deep breathing, E.P.L.R. or physical exercises which have no relationship to the active and passive phases. It must be remembered, however, that it is generally advisable that all phases be related in content and theme.

THE TRIAD OF INTONATION

The triad of intonation can be used in many ways and should reflect the objective of the lesson. If the passive phase is to be used for straightforward vocabulary drill, it is advisable to use it as follows:

	Chair	*Horse*	*Floating*	*Hit*	*Fit*
N.V.:	ch	ho	fl	h	f
Wh.:	ai	r	oat	i	i
L.:	r	se	ing	t	t

The teachers should notice that digraphs and blends are not separated so as to conform to the triad and that rhythm and intonation are the essential elements. Thus syllabication is taught incidentally by natural rhythm as in the word "floating," even if it does not always conform to the rules. The use of rhythm and intonation have the objectives of enhancing recall and conforming to the basic assumptions of automatic and intuitive learning as discussed earlier.

This trial of intonation can be used in the same way during the active phase for word drill except that a visual stimulus should be present first.

Example:

    A. Present a flash card—"Floating"

    B. Ask the child (children) to turn on their television camera in their head(s) and visualize the word.

    C. The teacher then spells it in the triad as suggested.

Chapter 8

HANS—A NEW BEGINNING

10-18-79

My, what a challenge this boy is going to be. He has built such a shell around himself, he panics when he sees a book or when the word "learning" is even mentioned. He thinks he has a disease and is sure he cannot be cured. But I assure you he will be cured. I told him how bright he is, and of course, I am now the "liar of the month" in his eyes.

I suggested we take a fantasy trip over his farm on the magic-white cloud. He thought I was crazy, so I said "okay," I'll go by myself and I did. The poor boy never tried this before and he was scared to death to see a grown-up lunatic flying high in the alpha state over his farm.

I then asked Hans to help me to write a story. He turned his back. Well, I am an expert on language experience, and he is not, so what do you expect! I think the topping on the cake was my request that he do some deep breathing exercises to help him relax. He cried and said, "This is dumb." But he knows I mean business and that I consider myself an authority on this subject.

When he left today, he refused to commit himself about whether to come back or not. But he also refused to say he wouldn't come back.

The following three chapters are dedicated to a fine young boy named Hans who, ever since he started school, has suffered the frustrations of not being able to learn in the same way other students do. He is bright, creative, and charming.

The reader should follow these chapters carefully since they describe Hans's progress from the beginning and provide many lesson ideas. But more importantly these chapters describe a boy changing into a happy learner as he begins to experience success in learning.

At the beginning of the story Hans is an identified learning disability student, nine years of age, who is currently placed in the third grade. He gets special help at school but cannot seem to learn by the fragmented approach being used. He is reading at a primer level and is extremely discouraged.

I hardly blame the poor child. Imagine learning to read by doing relaxation exercises, going on fantasy trips, writing silly stories, and listening to music while an idiot professor sings words.

I'm convinced that he'll be back. If for no reason but curiosity, he will give it another try.

A Fantasy Trip
(For Mind Calming and Imagery)

The white cloud exercise starts this way:

Imagine that you are lying on your back on the grass on a warm summer day and that you are watching the clear blue sky without a single cloud in it (pause). You are lying there very comfortably, very relaxed, quite happy with yourself (pause). You simply are enjoying the beauty of watching the clear, beautiful, blue sky (pause). As you are lying there completely relaxed, enjoying yourself (pause) way off on the horizon you note a tiny white cloud (pause). You are fascinated by the simple beauty of the small white cloud against the clear blue sky background (pause). The little white cloud starts to move slowly towards you (pause). You are lying there completely relaxed, very much at peace with yourself, watching the little white cloud slowly come toward you (pause). You are enjoying the beauty of the clear blue sky and the tiny white cloud (pause). Finally the little white cloud comes to a stop overhead (pause). Completely relaxed, you are enjoying this beautiful scene (pause). You are very relaxed, very much at home with yourself, and simply enjoying the beauty of the little white cloud in the blue sky (pause). Now become the little white cloud. Project yourself into it (pause). You are the little white cloud, completely diffused, puffy, relaxed, very much at home with yourself (pause). Now you are completely relaxed, your mind is completely calm (pause), you are pleasantly relaxed, ready to proceed with the lesson. (Or use as a vehicle for a fantasy trip.) (Schuster, Bordon and Gritton, 93, pp. 24–25)

The story Hans refused to acknowledge:

My Trip (Over Hans's Farm)

I saw two collies and two wiener dogs.
I saw a barn, a house, and two garages.
I saw five horses.

Enrichment Workshop
Lesson Plan: 1 The First Day
Date: 10-18-79

Objectives:
- A. Create Proper Treatment Environment
- B. Provide Relaxed Conditions
- C. Create Trust
- D. Create Heightened Memory
- E. Provide for Suggestion-Desuggestion
- F. Imagery Activity

Preparation Phase:
- A. Get Acquainted
- B. Breathing Exercises
- C. White Cloud
- D. Fantasy Trip

Active Phase:
- A. Write experience chart
- B. Read together
- C. Have child copy in own book for subsequent practice
- D. Create flash cards—Visualization Practice

Passive Phase:
- A. Creative presentation
  Present words (rhythm and intonation). Student sees words on flash card (note the integration from Phase I to Phase II).

10-19-79

I spoke briefly with Hans's mother today, as I wandered through the Psychology Department. She is a graduate student there. I asked about what Hans had said following our first session. She replied, "Well, he thinks it's all dumb and that you are a little weird. He is really enthused but also very frightened." As she walked on she said, "He will be there Tuesday for sure."

His reactions do not surprise me. This is a typical response from students who experience this approach for the first time. I have heard it over and over again.

10-23-79

Well, Hans did come back, but let me assure you his concept, my concept, and his mother's concept of enthusiasm are certainly thousands of miles apart. Hans was furious at his mother for making him come. His mother was disappointed that Hans did not want to come. I'm the only enthusiastic one in the bunch.

Enrichment Workshop
Lesson Plan: 2 Early Recall Pleasant Learning
Date: 10-23-79

Objectives:
    A. Develop Calm, Open Mind
    B. Suggest Easy Learning
    C. Provide Vehicle for Language Experience

Preparation Phase:
    A. Do muscle relaxation
    B. Do Early Pleasant Learning Recall

Active Phase:
    A. Write a story about the early pleasant learning experience
    B. Select words for visualization practice (word shapes)

Passive Phase:
    A. While Hans visualizes words, instructor drills words with pleasant, and varied intonations. (Use of rhythm and intonation is explained in Chapter 3.)

Hans is making a noble effort to resist treatment but his curiosity is aroused and he is wondering if I might not be right about him. My suggestions, "you're bright, learning is easy and you'll soon be feeling better about school," are starting to get through to him.

He settled down some when I sat next to him and did some muscle relaxation. I need this too by late in the day. I did the Early Pleasant Recall exercise with him and followed up with some language experience during the active session. He was asked to recall the "fun" time he had when he learned to ride a bike. That story follows:

Riding My Bike*

> I learned to ride my bike when I was eight. I learned on a friend's bike. I was excited about learning. It was fun.

There was a major breakthrough today. Hans actually closed his eyes and carried through on the visualization practice with a few words I selected from his story. I must sit side by side with him and do everything he does. I did sneak a "peek" and he was doing it. Hans won't commit himself openly yet but does whatever I ask as long as he thinks I won't notice. He is on the way to being a good learner.

We worked on the shapes of words during visualization today. We drew boxes around his words from the story. He chuckled about the word $\boxed{\text{garage}}$ because he said it reminded him of his wiener dogs.

During the passive session, Hans visualized words while I drilled him in some not too distinct intonations. I'm trying to break him in gently and have decided not to bring in music until he has accustomed himself to the techniques he has already been exposed to. Soon I will begin to train him to breathe rhythmically so I can begin to synchronize word drills with his breathing to facilitate memory. (The rationale for this is described in a following lesson.)

Early Pleasant Learning Recall

Pick some early pleasant learning situation, some time in your life previously when you were learning something that you realized you liked and you really enjoyed. This may be as early as several years of age when your mother was reading to you or it might be as recently as reading your best liked fiction story only a year ago. Everybody got one? (If not, wait.) Be back there again and find yourself enjoying learning. Think about where you were (pause). Was anyone with you (pause)? What was your attitude or how did you feel about what you were reading or learning (pause)? Now take a look at yourself in this learning situation and how your mouth and throat felt (pause). Recall now how your stomach felt (pause). Recall how your whole body felt (pause). Now think about the thoughts you were thinking (pause). Take a look at the eager feelings you had about learning and reading (pause). Maximize that feeling, hang onto it, and learn the material you are about to hear in exactly the same

---

*I wrote this story since Hans refused to give input. But, he did look and listen.

way. Retain that eagerness to learn and top memory skill. (Schuster,
Bordon and Gritton, 93, pp. 31)

This particular exercise is related to indirect suggestion and is
the recalling of a past pleasant learning experience. One must
caution that it is not age regression but rather the reliving of an
early, satisfying learning experience. The subject is asked to relive the experience in every way physically, emotionally, and as
sensorily as possible. Once this is accomplished it is suggested that
the student will learn just as easily and with as much pleasure in
the current situation.

Later Today — 10-23-79

A young graduate student from the Psychology Department
stopped by today because he is interested in doing a master's thesis
on the Lozanov Method. He will end up being a school psychologist.
As usual, I cannot talk to school psychologists for more than
seven minutes without getting into an all-out philosophical battle
with them. They just cannot imagine how I could possibly work
with a child without testing the "brains" out of a child first.

I know all of Hans's reading deficits. He has them all! His
learning expectancy is so shattered now that Hans cannot imagine
himself being a good, happy learner. When Tom (the graduate
student) comes to my office for his next conference, I am going to
force him to sit in my armchair and breathe rhythmically while I
read the following to him:

LEARNING EXPECTATION

While expectation of the learner appears to be of prime importance in the learning situation, it cannot be classified solely as a
facilitator of learning but also as an outcome of suggestion. As
mentioned earlier, expectation belongs not only to the student but
to the instructor. In other words, it is not only how the learner
feels in regard to his ability to learn but also how the instructor
perceives the ability of the student. This expectation is transmit-
ted verbally and nonverbally.

Leonard's book, *Education and Ecstacy* (57) is filled with ideas
that the human potential is greater than most educators at this
time even imagine. He demands that educators begin to recognize

this and consider learning as a delight and as life's very purpose, thus raising the learner's expectation.

Kelley (50) talks about the uniqueness of every individual and the special contribution each individual can make if he is allowed to function.

For some time educators have been concerned about curriculum development and its importance to motivation. Kelley (50) charges that our schools cherish conformity and teachers for centuries have striven to bring everyone through our schools knowing the same things; thus, perpetuating the idea that learning is a bore and as Katz (49) indicated, offering no motivation for sustained interest and effort.

Furthermore, students have been, according to Lozanov, Holt and others, lead to believe they are dumb and expectations are thus lowered and productivity hindered.

Frost and Rowland (35) state that each learner has acquired and is cued by expectancies of the supportive or the nonsupportive behavior of the drive structure, habit patterns, and expectancies. These authors support Goodlad's negative philosophies regarding the graded grouping plan, lock step curriculum, and promotion policies which bore the fast student and frustrate the slower learners. Coleman (25, p. 98) discusses the negative results of nonpromotion policies and its effect on the learner.

> He is likely, in contrast to his having been promoted, to have: a less healthy self-concept, take a more negative view of school, take part in fewer school activities, have fewer companions in his grade, and be viewed less favorably by his teacher.

The Lozanov method was designed, through positive suggestion, to raise the learner's expectancies and thus motivate him to learn better. It is designed, in particular, to desuggest the self-suggested or socio-suggested norms he has internalized or been cued to.

Once the expectations are raised, the entire suggestive process must be maintained. The aforementioned mechanisms and facilitators are designed to do just that. It is interesting to note that this subtle transmission of expectancy to the subjects is likened to the Hawthorne effect. Biehler (10, p. 21) calls it "the subtle and unintentional transmission of an expectancy of the experimenter to the subjects of a study," or the experimenter bias effect. This phenomenon was first identified by Roethlisberger and Dickson (83).

Rosenthal and Jacobson (85), in their book *Pygmalion in the*

Classroom, reported a study where students made significant gains in IQ standings because teacher expectations of certain pupils were raised. This phenomenon is explained by what is called self-fulfilling prophecy. In other words, "One person's prediction to another's behavior somehow comes to be realized. It is operated by teachers communicating their enthusiasm and faith to the pupil" (Biehler, 10, p. 23).

According to Biehler, Barber and Silver and others in their research discredit the impact of expectation. But, Biehler (10) merely suggests that neither the Hawthorne effect nor the Pygmalion effect are yet clearly established. It was further suggested here that in future research emphasis should not be put on whether expectancy exists but rather how they operate. They go on to suggest that educators must at least be aware that expectancies may lead to the "self-fulfilling prophecy."

Lozanov (64) in his approach supports the Hawthorne and Pygmalion effects and attempts to explain them through the science of suggestion. The aforementioned components of his method, when ap-applied properly in the classroom, are claimed to support the expectancy phenomenon as not only achievable, but maintainable. Other studies appear to give added support to his unique methodology.

10-29-79

What a marvelous child this boy is. He is handsome, bright, creative, and fun to be with. It's a pity that he feels he is a bore, dumb, and that he has very little to offer the world. I'm working hard to convince him otherwise. Once this happens the rest will follow.

It's becoming more and more obvious that this child will compensate only when he begins to believe in himself. Then he'll have to develop his own decoding system and he'll take off just like the rabbit in today's story.

Hans is very slowly beginning to get involved. He actually offered some input into today's story. What a thrill that was for both of us! I saw his eyes light up when he saw his own words come to life on the experience chart. I wrote his story for him. Although he offered only a few words, he took another giant step forward. I now think that he is barely reading at the primer level. Yet today, he learned the words bridge, nice, valley, mountain and a few others.

We took turns selecting words from his story to put on flash cards. Naturally he chose the words he knew and "naturally" I chose the words he didn't. Soon I'll know exactly "where he's at" without a test. (I must tell Tom about this!)

We practiced visualization again. Hans and I looked at words and then closed our eyes to see the words in "the mind's eye." Hans is good at this. "After all, he does have a hidden television camera in his brain." He is going to use that and whatever other brain power he can conjure up to learn to read. He has power in his mind and its tremendously creative. When we talked about the shape of the word rabbit, he said, "It looks like a city!" But it does and Hans proved it to me when he drew his picture of the word rabbit (rabbit).

During the passive session, I sang out his words in three levels of intonations. I can't wait until I can add rhythmic breathing because that added tool will step up his memory process. The plan for lesson three follows:

Enrichment Workshop
Lesson Plan: 3
Date: 10-29-79

Objectives:
  A. To provide for a calm mind.
  B. To provide for an open mind.
  C. To provide an "easy" learning environment.
  D. To break down learning barriers.
  E. To provide a vehicle of suggestion.

Preparation Phase:

  A. Do Mind Calming Activity
   1. Wave of Tension. (See page 73.)
   2. Mountain Climbing activity (number 2 is integrated into active phase with language experience).

Active Phase:

   Write a story about what we saw going up the mountain. Select new vocabulary from the story for visualization practice.

   Review old stories and vocabulary until the child knows them perfectly.

Passive Phase:

> Student will listen passively while the instructor spells
> out new words in varied intonations.

Hans's Story Today

Up the Mountain

> We climbed up the mountain. It was morning and a nice cool day. It was
> windy in the woods. As we entered the woods we saw a deer and a rabbit.
> In the valley we saw a bridge, a man and a car.

The Mountain Climbing Exercise

> Imagine you are climbing a mountain, you are near the top and it is
> just before dawn (pause). You are walking easily towards the top of the
> mountain and enjoying the scenery (pause). You are walking through a
> forest and about to come out to a clearing on top (pause). This is beautiful
> scenery around you and a beautiful view is about to unfold (pause). You
> are walking along quite easily just about at the top now, quite relaxed and
> comfortable (pause). The dawn is about to break on a pretty day (pause).
> Now you reach the top of the mountain and you see as you reach the top,
> the sun is just coming up (pause). You look down and see the first rays of
> the sun hitting the valley. It is a beautiful sight before you (pause). Now
> at the top of the mountain, you relax and enjoy yourself and really
> appreciate the beautiful view in front of you (pause). It's a very calm,
> beautiful scene; the sun is shining now brilliantly into the valley (pause).
> Although much of the valley is yet in shadow, it is beautifully illuminated.
> It is a very pretty scene (pause). Drink in the beauty of this scene. Enjoy
> it to the maximum (pause). Now get ready to learn the material for today
> with this same calm, peaceful feeling (pause). (Schuster, Bordon and
> Gritton, 93, p. 26.)

RATIONALE FOR MIND CALMING

Suggestibility is related, according to Lozanov, to the attitudes
and moods of the subjects. Following physical exercise to relax the
body, mind calming activities will further assure heightened
suggestibility.

One of the techniques discussed by Schuster (88) is Zen breathing.
It is merely paying attention to breathing as the subject inhales,
holds, and exhales. It is sometimes used as a preclass treatment to

assist pseudo-passivity or used during the teaching session. In this case, students breathe in unison and the presentation of material is often synchronized with it (Schuster and Hasbrook, 90). Lozanov holds that it enhances suggestibility and keeps the mind clear. That is, students will receive suggestions more easily when anxiety is not present, since these suggestions are directed toward ideas that learning is fun and easy.

According to Lindgren (59), anxiety is an emotional state characterized by fear, apprehension, or tension. It is also the anticipated fear of failure brought on possibly by former learning experiences. He feels that some anxiety is necessary because it leads to a wish to avoid anxiety and thus the individual learns to be careful and considerate in his relationships to others and conforms to laws and customs of the society. Our anxiety, however, leads to a negative direction in human development and causes one to dwell on avoidance of anxiety and thus reducing productivity. Lindgren (59) insists that every action one makes is carefully calculated to avoid anxiety or at least to forestall it.

While Lozanov attempts to totally desuggest anxiety in the learning setting, Sullivan (102) feels it would be overprotective to shield the child from all that is negative. It appears that it is not Lozanov's purpose to shield but rather to comply with the critical barriers to suggestion and learning that already exist.

Lindgren (59, p. 278) states:

> One of the outstanding characteristics of experienced teachers is their ability to sense the anxiety level in the classroom group. They are aware that little learning will take place if the group is more concerned about its anxiety than it is about learning.

There is further support of this concept. To paraphrase Flanders (33), students who are anxious often give the problem of anxiety priority over the learning task at hand.

Lindgren also suggests teachers can assist students in overcoming anxiety in the classroom by having a gripe session, changing the scene or restructuring the learning situation. It appears that these tactics might merely result in reconstructing or reorganizing the anxiety. The gripe session appears, in itself, to be negative and could suggest further anxiety in the student.

Once physical relaxation is accomplished, mind calming exercises should be pursued. Schuster, Bordon, and Gritton (93) suggest some excellent mind-calming exercises in their teaching manual: Zen breathing (which has already been discussed) white cloud, and climbing the mountain exercises.

Added Information

Many concepts have already been applied in Hans's case. The following explanations will assist the reader in grasping a broader understanding of these concepts. Chapters 3 and 4 will also be of value.

IMAGERY AND SENSORY ELEMENTS

It is common in the Lozanov methodology for the instructor to suggest that students develop deep imagery and sensory feelings about what is being taught. According to Lozanov, this facilitates learning and aids retention.

Strang (100, p. 29) defines imagery as the ability to create mental images or "to see it in the mind's eye." According to Strang, imagery has been referred to with many terms: visual memory, mental imagery, inner perception, reperception and visualization. Strang cites Radaker's studies in 1962 regarding the importance of imagery to memory: fourth grade social studies students were given practice in assignments containing vivid descriptions whereby they had to describe, in writing, mental pictures created and do illustrations about them. The students who had imagery practice consistently did better on memory tests than control groups not having this practice. The Stanford-Binet Memory for Designs Test and the Graham and Kendall Memory Tests were used.

Dilley (30, p. 110) supports mental imagery (M.I.) as a powerful tool, "Mental imagery can be a powerful ally in personal efforts to achieve life's goals." He goes on to state that mental imagery not only develops the memory but is a tool for reducing fear and aiding relaxation. He suggests imagining as sensorily as possible "a favorite place" to relieve tension.

Dilley (30) in his article also discusses the use of M.I., to improve memory, that goes as far back as Cicero. Cicero recommended an association approach of vividly imagining familiar objects in a certain sequence and then associating unfamiliar things one needs to memorize with the familiar. Dr. Dilley cites other researchers who recognize the power of M.I. and its value in memory growth, relaxation and desensitization, i.e., Maltz (66).

Montessori (68) assigns great importance to sensory functions as a process through which a child lays the foundations of intelligence by receiving sensations from his environment and thereby making observations, comparisons, and judgments.

Accordingly, a person becomes acquainted with the environment and develops intelligence. Lozanov, likewise, puts importance on sensory activity for creating vivid imagery as a memory aid. The imagery desired is to be pleasant and sensory enough so the subject develops strong feelings about what is being taught and assures meaningfulness.

Beery (9) states that words with pleasant and meaningful associations are more easily learned. Lindgren (59) proposes that material be presented in a way that allows students to make their own vivid associations with minimum help from the teacher. This involvement enables materials to gain a degree of importance to the learner and enhances retention.

According to Johnson and Myklebust (46) imagery, as a process, has been neglected in education and psychology. Imagery pertains to sensation and information that has already been perceived and received. He considers imagery as one process of memory in which the student is recalling not only sounds but making visualizations. The inability to do so, according to Myklebust, hinders the memory process.

Schuster (88) in his research has documented that when students are told to fully experience new words being taught, they appear to learn them better. The added feature to this approach according to Lozanov is that students become more perceptive and stimulated.

RELAXATION TECHNIQUES

The primary objective of this approach is to induce a state of openness to suggestion, and thus learning, during the teaching session. Physical relaxation, according to some researchers, is a must since it precedes a calm relaxed mind. Studies by Chaney and Andreasen (22) indicate that students' recall on random numbers was significantly better when physical relaxation exercises preceded the memorization session.

Kline (53) in his experimentation with physical and mental relaxation found Silva Mind Control methods effective when working with students. In his experiments at Sandy Springs School, Sandy Springs, Maryland, Kline found students more receptive to materials presented following Silva Mind Control exercises.

Astor (2) recommends meditation and relaxation to reach transcendence, or higher levels of expectation and performance. The concept of transcendence in education is not new. Maslow (67) described it as "peaking" or a transcendence of dichotomies, polarities, and conflicts.

One of Lozanov's (64) objectives for the state of relaxation during the learning session is to produce a calm mind devoid of fear. While he does not use meditative approaches, it is recommended by Astor, Nidich, Greaves and others to increase control and reduce fear (Nidich, Seeman and Dreskin, 71).

Lozanov (64) encourages physical exercise prior to or during the learning lesson itself. This recommendation for muscle tension exercises has the purpose of inducing relaxation rather than the "muscle education" concept as proposed by Montessori (68), although it could have similar effects.

Blitz (11) states that good teachers recognize the need for periodic release of physical tension by allowing intermittent periods of physical exercise for their students. These are usually informally prescribed activities to quiet students and help them tune in and listen to the lesson. Lozanov suggests that external passiveness produces internal superactivity of the mind.

Some exercises that appear to be effective are bend-overs, side bends, turtle-neck exercises, whole body tension and others.

The following exercises are suggested by Schuster, Bordon, and Gritton (93) as preliminary exercises.

PHYSICAL EXERCISES

Bend-overs

Students are asked to stand erect and touch their toes or come as close as possible; three attempts are sufficient.

Side bends

Students are requested to stand erect and move sideways, reaching down as far as possible. Some will be able to reach the knees or even further, without bending them. This exercise should take place three times on both the right and the left sides.

Turtle-neck

First the students are asked to tense the left side of the neck, then the right side and lastly, the center. This exercise should be done sequentially three times. Students are then asked to drop their heads to the chest in a relaxed way and pull back up in a tensed way. This exercise is repeated three times.

The third part of the turtle-neck exercise involved having the subject tense his neck moderately and turn it clockwise and counterclockwise in a relaxed way to relieve tension.

Whole body tension

Subjects are asked to put their hand out directly in front of them and tense the whole body. Once the body is completely tensed, subjects move their arms from the front to the sides maintaining the tension. Tension is not relaxed until the hands are returned to the front position. Again, this should be repeated three times.

Hewitt (39) recommends "step-by-step" exercises that begin with the lower legs, induce tension, and then release. One then moves on to the upper legs inducing and releasing tension, one leg at a time. The subject moves upward through all of the body, one set of muscles at a time, until the top of the head is reached. This is all accomplished in a prone position. Schuster, Bordon, and Gritton (93) suggest a wave of tension exercise which would appear to be less time consuming and more practical in the classroom setting. It is accomplished by beginning with the feet and inducing tension in all sets of muscles simultaneously until the top of the head is reached. The entire body is held in tension a few seconds and then released. This exercise can be accomplished three times in approximately fifteen to twenty seconds.

Summary Statements

The following summary statements will prepare the reader before going on to the next chapters and Hans's future lessons.

Hans

This nine-year-old third grader is currently reading at a primer level. He is extremely "uptight" about learning and views himself as being stupid. He is actually above average and highly creative. He cannot learn to read by the traditional methods. His program at school is phonetic in nature and for whatever reasons, Hans cannot learn that way. His repeated failures have caused deep anxiety and created intense learning barriers which must be desuggested. He has failed to compensate because his educational program at school does not allow him to develop his own personalized decoding system.

The above appears to be true for many students who are having learning problems. They are bombarded day after day, year after year with the same old program. Consequently, the psychological problems become greater than whatever factors caused the child's initial learning difficulties. To break through the learning barriers and assist the child in developing his own learning system one must keep the following in mind:

  A. The primary objective is affective in nature and designed to desuggest the learning barriers.

  B. The approach is totally holistic with absolutely no phonics being taught except in a very indirect way. The teacher allows the child to make his own phonetic associations if he needs them. In place of phonics, word visualization drills are used along with exercises to improve memory.

  C. By stressing the creative and affective aspects of the lesson one suggests very indirectly that that is more important than reading and the child then relaxes his defenses. Thus learning to read is an automatic outcome *not* a direct objective.

  D. Activities from preparation phase, to active and passive phases are carefully integrated into a meaningful, collective whole.

  E. The assumption is made by the teacher that the child is bright and can learn very easily. This is suggested over and over again, directly and indirectly, to the child. The teacher *must* believe this so that the child will raise his expectations.

F. Facilitators of memory and suggestion as described in the text of Hans's lessons and future chapters must be adhered to.

The next three chapters will focus in on the three lesson phases in greater depth. While there is notable repetition, it will give the reader a broader understanding of the available alternatives.

Chapter 9

HANS—SELF-DISCOVERY

Ihaven't seen Hans for over a week because we gave "each other" the flu.

Hans's mother spoke to me several days ago and expressed her pleasure over changes she has seen in Hans. "He seems to feel better about himself and now looks forward to his sessions with you." This is good news and he is responding right on schedule. It does take several weeks before children begin to accept the new approach and to begin to believe that they will learn. Now, I can slowly begin to train him in other techniques to accelerate his learning!

Ostrander and Schroeder (73) cite considerable evidence that rhythmic breathing is valuable for increasing memory. The use of music is also helpful during the passive session. These concepts are explained in detail later on in this chapter.

Since Hans is learning to read using a whole word approach anything one can use to facilitate memory will be of great value to him.

Today's Lesson

Hans arrived a few minutes late and not too excited. The time lapse since his last lesson was in evidence and it is so easy to fall back into the old trap that holds one captive.

It was my intention to begin working on his new biography. After the preliminaries, we were to discuss his favorite hero. Then I had planned to incorporate the qualities he admired in this person into a "new name" for Hans. But unfortunately (for my glorious lesson, only), he could only come up with Mazinga the robot as his favorite hero. I don't want Hans to be a robot who might or might not be able to read. So I used his enthusiasm about Mazinga to write another story.

Hans now gives enthusiastic input into the language experience stories. At the beginning he would not offer a word, but now he beams as I write his words down for him.

During the preparation phase we did a Zen breathing type of exercise followed by the white cloud mind calming activity. I interject the positive suggestions as we proceed: "This lesson will be easy, you are a bright boy, reading is easy and fun." Hans no longer thinks I'm a liar.

Enrichment Workshop
Lesson Plan: 4
Date: 11/12/79

Objectives:

    A. To provide for a calm mind.
    B. To reduce learning phobia.
    C. To improve self-image.
    D. To provide a vehicle of suggestion.
    E. To provide a vehicle for language experience.

Preparation Phase:

    A. Breathing exercise.
    B. White cloud.
    C. Positive suggestion.

Active Phase:

    A. Discuss favorite hero.*
    B. Write a brief story about favorite hero.
    C. Do word visualization with problem words from the story.

Passive Phase:

    A. Present problem words through triad of intonation.

---

*I felt it best not to accept Mazinga the robot as his favorite hero. But we wrote about him anyway.
Note: Old stories are reviewed each day by partner reading even though it is seldom mentioned. Do it in active phase or following the passive.

Today's Story

Mazinga

He is as tall as a skycraper and about that strong. He is a robot and chases bad robots and destroys them. Also Mazinga can fly at the speed of sound.

He has a sword to get out of traps.

So intense is Hans's word phobia that he does not attempt to apply any phonics to his reading. I asked him how he can tell the difference between a squirrel and a bear when he goes into the forest. We discussed this at length. I made no attempt to discuss phonics but told him that words have shapes and characteristics too. Furthermore one does not have to see the whole word to recognize it. I illustrated that by drawing the picture of the top half of a squirrel. Hans must not be pressured into using any particular type of word recognition technique. Since it is now necessary that he develop his own personalized system.

Today's lesson went very well and I am pleased to see his raised spirits. He now has hope and has developed some belief in himself. I must be careful not to lose patience, or faith in him for even a moment. Children are so perceptive to the teacher's true feelings. Hans cannot possibly believe in himself unless he truly perceives that his teacher shares that belief. This concept is vital to the maintenance of positive learning expectation.

November 16 & 20, 1979

I will share the lesson plan for the above two days. It is necessary frequently to provide for meaningful review, so one lesson was set aside for this. The format for the lesson stays the same along with all preliminary mind calming activities and positive suggestion.

Enrichment Workshop
Lesson Plan: 5 & 6
Date: 11/ 16, 20 /79

Objectives:

    A. Provide for a calm, open mind.

    B. Suggest easy learning.

    C. Review words.

    D. Provide for visual memory development.

Preparation Phase:

    A. Mountain climbing exercise.

    B. Attentive breathing.

    C. Suggest easy learning and good memory.

Active Phase:

    A. Using words from the four stories we have written so far. We will write a nonsense story.

    B. Partner reads the new story several times.

Passive Phase:

    A. Work on words through visualization. (See visual stimulus, close eyes to form the word in the mind's eye.)

Our Review Story

Mazinga's Attack

We were walking up the mountain. Suddenly we saw Mazinga fly over us and the mountain. It gave me a tickling feeling. I was excited. He was going to destroy Germany.

I have been perfectly thrilled by Hans's progress during the past six lessons. He has learned many new words and now recognizes them in context and an ever increasing number in isolation. This is a giant step forward for Hans.

November 21, 1979

For some weeks I have been waiting for the best time to introduce other instructional tools into Hans's session. These will provide further variety as well as serving many other objectives. These are as follows: Psychodrama, music, and rhythmic breathing. (Thus far we have engaged only in deep breathing). The rationale for use of psychodrama follows.

PSYCHODRAMA

Psychodrama is an important part of the Lozanov method. It is the reinforcement used not only to strengthen memory of what has been learned but also to provide for creative stimulation and group interaction. Lindgren (59) has indicated that reinforcement of what has been taught is important to retention but goes on to shun meaningless, repetitious drill. In accordance with this thinking, Lozanov recommends creative activity as a vehicle of practice.

Numerous writers have spoken about the importance and power of creativity in the classroom. E. Paul Torrance (106) feels that nothing could contribute more to our nation, satisfaction and mental health of our people than creative behavior. It needs to be energized and guided from birth. Joyce (47, p. 403) recommends creative activity in the classroom. "Where the classroom climate is open and encourages the unusual and the creative, then what kind of behavior is likely to flourish."

Lozanov (64) recommends role playing skits, plays and games as the proper reinforcement tools and at the same time foster creativity and a relaxed learning atmosphere.

Joyce (47, p. 176) calls role playing, "The enactment of situations by individuals. The participants act out social situations designed to help them open up specific aspects of interpersonal relations." It can be used, he goes on to say, for skill and attitude development and many other purposes. Lozanov often assigns students new names and new roles to play to reduce inhibition.

Since much of Lozanov's experimentation with his method has been in the teaching of foreign languages, role playing appears to be a natural way to practice dialogues and at the same time act out situations, feelings, and provide for group interaction. Joyce (47) points out that instructional material can provide the information but it is the teaching strategy that assures meaningfulness and true understanding. Joyce (47, p. 399) goes on to state that "game-type simulations provide a good setting for testing whether students can apply knowledge, principles and theories to real life social situations."

Creative dramatics are used most frequently in the Lozanov method as reinforcement for material learned and for the purpose of fostering a creative atmosphere. This concept is not new in western education. Ruth Strickland (101, p. 458) had this to say about the value of creative dramatics:

> Drama, especially for older children, involves people and their behavior and emotions. In playing a part the child steps out of himself, his own personality and into the personality of someone else. He is freed from his own limitations and inhibitions.

Hudnut (41) also gives support to what Lozanov calls psychodrama when he said, "The creative impulse, which is concerned with making and doing, gives direction and meaning to our activities and transforms life into an art."

There appear to be strong implications in the above statement in that it might be ineffective for teachers to direct learning activities for the purpose of conformity. Some researchers feel that rigidity in the learning climate might be more detrimental than helpful since all learners have their own field perceptions and must act them out accordingly. Some modern researchers who are attempting to support this contention are Kelley (50) and Combs and Purkey (27).

MUSIC

Music is used extensively to facilitate rhythm in the presentation and to provide for a more creative learning style. Presentation of material is often, but not necessarily, orchestrated with the time of the music. Music containing sixty beats per minute is often used in presentation with selections from Bach or Mozart. Intonation is often coupled with this rhythm as the instructor raises and lowers his voice as the content is being presented.

Use of music in instruction is not, of course, a new concept in this country and has a strong rationale that is not unlike Lozanov's. Siks (95, p. 157) can be quoted as saying:

> Music has power. It arouses feelings that surge through old and young alike. Marching music almost always quickens the blood, stirs imaginations and causes an irrepressible urge to move into action. Lullabies are soothing in their gentle rhythm and have a quieting effect. Music stirs many different feelings.

Music also has the effect, according to Siks, of motivating or suggesting a specific environment and arouses thinking and feeling.

Lozanov recommends the creative presentation as a way not only to maintain pseudo-passiveness but to raise expectation. As Siks concludes, music is always associated with such events as parades, the circus, rodeos, parties and festivities. Materials that center in an imaginative realm may be heightened by music which provides a mood as well as a rhythmic pattern.

Lozanov (64) does not suggest that music alone provides for easier memorization. But he hypothesizes that it is also the rhythmic presentation of material that increases volume of learning. Schleicher (87) states that music distracts the learner's attention, thus, opening a direct route to the brain. Music, therefore, is just a facilitator.

December 5, 1979

A miracle is happening to Hans. Too much time had again lapsed between the time he had his last lesson and today's lesson. But in spite of this, Hans remembered every single word he had been exposed to. He arrives at class now with a smile and leaves with one. His smile says "Hope" and that means that half the battle has already been won. I can't believe that he is the same boy that came to me such a short time ago.

Academically speaking, he is beginning to accelerate. Hans's memory is improving and he is beginning to compare likes and differences between words he is learning. At first it appeared that he concerned himself only with syntax and his ability to predict what the next word could be. This is a powerful tool. He then moved on to word shapes and now is beginning to evaluate words in relation to their phonetic elements. This is a very natural process and need not be taught. As mentioned before, Hans must develop his own personalized decoding system and this can happen only if the teacher does not interfere.

Thus far, his most notable improvement is affectively oriented. The rest will follow in time—his time, not mine!

It is always a good idea to have an alternate plan available for each lesson. Again my attempt to begin the new biography (new name) failed. Hans has not, at this point, identified strongly with anyone. I must help him do that first. Most students I have worked with have a well-developed hero worship system from which to draw. The teacher can then build from that and attempt to transfer all the good qualities of the hero into the student. But, for now, this must wait.

Lesson six involved a continuation of Hans's passion for robots. We did the white cloud exercise during the preparation phase with suggestions of good health, memory, and self-esteem. During the active session we reviewed all of his new words and wrote a new story.

Giant Robot

> I'd like to be like a giant robot because he guards people. He has tough fingers and skin. He can fly. He does his own orders. He is about six stories tall. He sacrificed his life for the earth.

This story permeates with Hans's need for strength, protection, and freedom. These are all necessary for the process of self-actualization and should be viewed as being very natural. During the passive session I pulled new words from the story for visual practice.

I still feel the need to wait a short time before introducing more elements into the lesson. I am ready to use music during the passive session, but I'm not sure Hans is. This is still all so new to him that I want him to feel perfectly comfortable with our current approach before introducing any other component.

December 7, 1979

Hans came in beaming today ready to go to work. After the preliminaries he reread his story about the giant robot. He said he didn't like it. When I asked why, he replied, "It just doesn't make sense." That's great! So we rewrote his story as follows and added one more chapter to it.

Giant Robot

Chapter 1

> I'd like you to hear about Giant Robot. He has hard fingers and skin. He can fly. He does his own orders. He is about six stories high. He risked his life for the earth.

Chapter 2

He fought creatures from another planet. To name one of them, there is one called Giant Eye. After he destroyed Giant Eye, Zombie flew in. Giant Robot grabbed him and flew away into space and hit a meteor. Both of them were destroyed.

Two beautiful things emerged from Hans today. First, he refused to let me have any input into his story. The stories now have to be entirely his. This is an important step forward. It shows great progress in his feeling of security in the reading act.

Secondly, he said he does not want to be like Giant Robot because he is not real. Finally, Hans is ready to join the human race. What a thrill today's lesson was for both of us.

Today's Lesson
Lesson Plan: 7
Date: 12/7/79

Objectives:
    A. To develop a calm mind.
    B. To suggest easy learning.
    C. To build self-esteem.

Preparation Phase:

    A. Deep breathing.
    B. Mountain climbing exercise.
    C. Suggestions: You are now relaxed. Your mind is open. Your memory is improving. Learning is easy for you.

Active Phase:

    A. Change story about Giant Robot.
    B. Wrote Chapter Two of Giant Robot.

Passive Phase:

    A. Word visualization using new words from the story.
    B. I sang words to him while he had visual images of the words.

An Imagery Experience

by Carol Forward (Graduate Student)

Imagine yourself sitting beside a river on a beautiful warm fall day. The wind is blowing gently against the colorful autumn leaves. (Pause) Watch them. (Pause) Smell them. (Pause) That's right, take a deep breath and inhale fall's fresh air.

Now slowly walk toward the river's edge. (Pause) Listen to the sound of the crisp leaves crunching beneath your feet. (Pause) Now stand still and watch the water drifting by with reflections of the trees dancing on. (Relax)

Quickly look up! Something's falling from the sky. Why, it's only a leaf falling from the tree above. Watch another twirl its way to the river. (Pause) And another . . . dances by you.

Now allow yourself to become one of those leaves hanging on gently to the tree's arm. (Pause) Feel the wind blowing against you high up in the tree. Whoops! The wind has blown you from the tree and you are twirling to the ground. (Pause) The wind blows a little harder and you are drifting towards the river. (Pause) Land softly on the river's surface.

Now you are drifting downstream. On and on you float down the river. (Pause) Relax, watch the clouds go by, relax and listen to mother nature's sounds. (Pause) Shortly you will come to a sharp bend in the river. Be ready for it. A special adventure awaits you there. Close your eyes. (Pause) See what's ahead in your mind. (Pause) Now open your eyes and tell about your adventure.

December 11, 1979

It is time to add something new to the lessons. This will prevent boredom and give Hans additional word and memory power.

Today's Lesson*
Lesson Plan: 8
Date: 12/11/79

Objectives:
  A. To develop a calm, open mind.
  B. To continue to bring about extinction of learning barriers.
  C. To develop hero worship concepts.
  D. Develop rhythmic breathing.

---

*Each lesson has many unwritten objectives. It is usually necessary to write only those which are central to the lesson on a particular day.

E. Develop imagery at fantasy level.

F. Develop imagery at the word visualization level.

Preparation Phase:

A. Rhythmic breathing (inhale 1, 2, 3, 4 — exhale 1, 2, 3, 4)

B. New imagery experience (example follows today's lesson).

C. Suggestion: Better memory, self-image, easy and fun learning.

D. Use of music to enhance passivity and suggestion.

Active Phase*

A. Review stories.

B. Make flash cards of words still causing problems.

C. Do word visualization practice.

Passive Phase†

A. Review all known and new words by the following process:

Student — Looks at word and inhales — 1, 2, 3, 4 — closes eyes to exhale and visualize word.

Teacher — Presents words visually on inhale — 1, 2, 3, 4 — sings word in three triads of intonation during exhale cycle, while student closes his eyes to do mental visualization.

Discussion of Lesson Eight

Hans arrived full of enthusiasm and satisfaction today. He practiced eight new words at home. He recalled six of them when we drilled during the latter part of the active phase. What a thrill for him to know lots of words that many other third graders could not identify.

Hans is now taking his experience charts home and copying them in his notebook. I have one of our secretaries type them for the book he is writing.

Time went so fast that we did not get into the passive phase so lesson nine will be a continuation of this lesson.

---

*The new imagery experience will be used only to develop a calm state of mind and vehicle of suggestion. A story will be written around it during a later lesson.

†Music will be added today without explanation except to say that it is relaxing. Actually it is used to maintain the suggestive, calm atmosphere.

Hans groaned a little when we did the rhythmic breathing introduction. It was "a this is dumb" kind of groan, but he went along with it.

Lesson: 9
December 14, 1979

Lesson plan eight outlined the objectives for this continuation. We will engage in mind calming by using the river exercise and practice rhythmic breathing again. The suggestions will again be geared toward good memory and easy learning.

Hans really enjoys the music we play during the passive sessions. If I fail to turn it on he will ask me if he can.

After doing the river relaxation exercise we practiced word visualization combined with rhythmic breathing as described in lesson eight.

Hans accepted this procedure quite well but will have to practice a number of times before it will become effective.

Lesson Plan: 9
December 18, 1979

Objectives:
  - A. Mind calming activities.
  - B. Bring about extinction of the learning barrier.
  - C. Provide for a vehicle of suggestion.

Preparation Phase:
  - A. Do the river relaxation exercise.

Active and Passive Phase:

  - A. We reviewed old stories Hans had written and played games with his new words, so as to provide more exposures.

January 9, 1980

Today we open up a new year in Hans's life. He came into my office bubbling over with enthusiasm about everything that had transpired over his Christmas vacation.

I was ill prepared for him since my work has piled up over the holidays. So I had Hans help me gather materials and lay out some plans for the coming weeks.

We reviewed one of his stories. He had forgotten only three words in his story, "the Crab and Spider I Built." This brightened both his day and mine. It added even further credibility to what we are both striving for. I'm striving to constantly improve the method while he is battling the scars of lifelong feelings of insecurity and failure.

Lesson: 10
January 14, 1980

Objectives:
   A. To create a calm mind.
   B. To improve self-image.
   C. To provide a vehicle for suggestion.
   D. To provide for content.

Preparation Phase:

   A. Deep breathing exercise.
   B. White cloud exercise. (Use as mind calming and vehicle for a fantasy trip.)

Active Phase:

   A. Review stories from the experience journal.
   B. Write story on fantasy trip.
   C. Put problem words on flash cards.

Passive Phase:

   A. Do visualization practice with problem words from new story.

Special Notes

A marvelous thing happened today. Hans said he wanted to take a trip by taking over himself. We started out with the white cloud exercise. Once we were both up in the cloud, he took over and directed us toward our destination. He did a marvelous job. It appears that our next story is going to be a long and interesting one. We are preparing for a long-term space flight. Chapter One of Hans story follows.

The Journey to the Space Station

We flew to Houston control by the ocean. We talked to the chief of staff. He hired us. He sent us (Hans and two friends) to an office near his. The adults went to an office behind him. (Me and whoever else Hans later decides will go on the journey.)

We had three boxes of starbird. One box had a landing base and the other had space ships. One was black and short the other one long and white. The white one had an escape capsule. (We are going to build a model space station before embarking on our journey.)

Lesson: 11
January 18, 1980

Objectives:

A. To intensify the effort to bring about the further extinction of learning barriers.
B. To provide for content material.

Preparation Phase:

A. Deep breathing exercise. (Hans is now resisting rhythmic breathing.)
B. Do white cloud to continue our journey and provide for content of today's story.

Active Phase:

A. Reread latest story.
B. Write next chapter of "The Journey to the Space Station."
C. Review old vocabulary using background music and word visualization.

Special Notes

I have now gathered enough evidence regarding Hans's best learning modes that we should be able to accelerate his learning considerably. He has now overcome many of his overt fears in relation to learning. His learning barriers are beginning to break down, but are still not near enough to extinction to relax the procedure. The following appear to have great value for Hans:

    A. Relaxation exercises.
    B. Positive suggestion.
    C. The language experience approach.
    D. Word visualization.
    E. A program *without* word attack skills. (I see evidence that he is now developing his own decoding system.)

I am now planning to step up the word drills using words in isolation. These words will come from his own stories.

Hans, at this time, needs about fifteen exposures to words before they become instant sight words. I must find as many ways to provide this as possible.

January 21, 1980

The glorious lesson I had planned for today had to be put off until the next time we meet. Hans came into my office today with a request that had to be granted immediately. Hans wanted to go to the library to find some books that "maybe" we could read together. This is a historic event in Hans's life.

We chose five books on the topic of outer space and the history of space travel. I will now begin to include the use of books in his lessons mainly through partner reading and writing about what he reads.

Lesson: 12
January 25, 1980

Objectives:
    A. To bring about further extinction of learning barriers.
    B. To develop imagery and word visualization abilities.
    C. To appreciate books.

Preparation Phase:
    A. Use the new imagery experience, "Once Upon A Tree," to develop a calm, open mind. (See the following.)
    B. Induce positive suggestion (i.e., your memory has improved, you have become a good student).

Active Phase:

A. Continue on space story.

B. Do word drill to determine which words still need practice through the visualization procedure.

C. Do some partner reading.

D. Word visualization with problem words. (See word. Close eyes and visualize.)

Passive Phase:

A. With use of music, words will be sung in the triad of intonation with visual exposure* for the student.

Once Upon A Tree — by a graduate student.

Get in a comfortable position so you can relax. Imagine you are a tree . . . a tall oak tree . . . standing all alone on a hill. The sun is shining on your branches and leaves. It feels so warm. The wind is softly blowing thru your leaves. You are standing so tall and straight . . . the sun feels so warm . . . the breeze is slowly moving your leaves. You are so tall you can see for miles. The sun is relaxing you as you look down on the country around you. You are standing so tall and so relaxed your mind begins to drift back. As you stand so tall and look around the country you remember . . . when you were just a young tree . . . so little on the top of this hill . . . only eight feet tall . . . you remember the day (time) that the Indians camped next to you. They used your tiny trunk to tie the spotted horse to. You watched them build their campfire and make their meals. The women tended the young ones so close by. (Continue in any manner to suit the subject.)

Summary

This concludes another chapter in Hans's life. I am immensely happy with his progress both affectively and academically. His mother summed things up very well yesterday when she said, "Hans is finally seeing himself in a new light and at last seeing words as whole meaningful things. He is no longer lost in a sea of parts and pieces." Isn't that beautiful!

---

*Usually I do not use the visual channels during the passive phase, but Hans often asks to look at the word rather than merely visualize it.

Chapter 10

A NEW BOY EMERGES

January 24, 1980

From Where to Where:

It has now been five months since Hans and I began helping each other learn to make sense out of reading. He has grown far more than I have lately, although I am picking up more techniques each week which fit the concept of the intuitive approach, I am also more convinced each day that these techniques are far more effective than the traditional ones for severely affected students.

Hans has blossomed here, at school and at home. The use of positive suggestion is certainly effective in his case and others I have worked with. While his learning inhibitions are not completely extinct in all settings, he no longer exhibits the telltale marks of task avoidance techniques while we are working together. This will eventually transfer to other learning-teaching situations to an even greater extent than it already has. To summarize Hans's progress thus far I would like the reader to be aware of the following:

A. Hans is beginning to view himself as a bright, worthy boy with a good future.

B. He is happier at home and in his school setting.

C. He no longer views reading as an activity dangerous to his ego structure.

D. Hans's memory has improved.

E. Hans is showing every evidence of developing his own decoding system. This is strongly evidenced by the fact that he now sees whole words, and is beginning to sound them out on his own. But far more important, he is becoming meaning oriented. I am not sure exactly how he is decoding, but I will certainly not interfere with it by battering him with phonic lessons.

F. Hans is now ready for the printed page. At his request, I am now reading with him from easy books related to his own interests (mainly space travel).

Current and Future Lessons

Hans's lessons now broaden to the use of books and other activities such as field trips and science experiments. The overall approach, however, will not change. The objectives for each lesson will continue to be affectively oriented and his academic growth will continue to be considered an automatic (intuitive) outcome of quality experiences. These will continue without change as will lesson sequence and we will continue with mind calming, imagery and visualization practice, positive suggestion, language experience, dramatic word drills and creative activity, as long as it is needed.

As time goes on, more psychodrama will be introduced into the lessons so that Hans can begin to play a more active role instead of the passive one. In addition the lesson content will be expanded with science lessons, social studies, and other areas of interests. The former practice with fantasy trips and the preceding imagery activity allow the teacher to broaden the use of this concept. Not only can one take fantasy trips, but one can incorporate word visualization along with it. This technique allows the child to experience some emotional impact with new words. It has the result of focusing away from word attack becoming "meaning" oriented.

Bobbing Bottle—by a graduate student

Imagine that it is a warm, sunny, summer day, and you have gone alone to a beach beside an ocean for a relaxing afternoon. You are lying on the beach very comfortably, very relaxed, just watching the waves roll in. (pause) You are watching the waves gently rolling in. (pause) You are perfectly relaxed, (pause) at peace with yourself and the world. (pause) As you are watching the waves gently roll in, you are interested to see a bottle floating in the water. (pause) You watch it bob slowly up and down as it comes with the waves toward shore. (pause) When it reaches shore, you go over and pick it up. (pause) Inside is a message which says, "If you find this bottle, please throw it back in the water." (pause) You carefully put the message back in the bottle and put the cork in tightly. (pause)

Then you throw it as hard as you can, and as far as you can, back out into the ocean. (pause) You watch as the ocean currents begin to pull the bottle back out to sea. (pause) You sit down and watch the bottle gently bobbing up and down. (pause) You are enjoying the warm sunshine, perfectly relaxed, just watching the bottle slide gently up and down the ocean waves. (pause) You are at peace with yourself, relaxed, enjoying watching the bottle get smaller as it gets farther and farther away. (pause) As you watch the bottle, it seems as if you are being pulled toward it. (pause) You seem to float towards it over the water. (pause) You are going with the bottle as it gently floats out to sea. (pause) You are sitting on the cork of the bottle, gently riding up and down the ocean waves. (pause) You are very relaxed, at peace with yourself, enjoying the warm sunshine and gentle waves. (pause) After a considerably long time, you feel the bottle again being drawn toward shore. (pause) You watch with interest as you get nearer to shore. (pause) You have gently washed up on shore. (pause) You leave the bottle and explore this place you have landed.

After giving adequate time "for exploration," return the child to the bottle. The tide washes it out to sea. The currents or wind return it to the home beach. You continue to describe the gently rolling waves and warm sunshine on the return trip.

Moon Flight — by a graduate student

Imagine you are flying to the moon. You are near takeoff. Your thoughts are mixed, as no one has ever ventured this far. The engines are roaring. (pause) You feel the shaking of the rocket. (pause) It shakes more and more. The countdown begins. . . . ten, nine, eight, seven, six, five, four, three, two, one. . . . Blast Off!! (pause) It takes you a few minutes to gather your thoughts. Your mind is reaching the moon and seeing its unique beauty. Each minute you're in this rocket, you dream of walking on the moon. (pause) This is your destiny (pause). . . . the moon. The radio sounds (pause) the moon is near! Landing gear ready? Ready. . . . land. You're landed! You get out of the rocket. Oh what beauty. (pause) It's so peaceful here. No people, no sounds, just quiet. You walk very slowly. What excitement! (pause) Craters upon craters. Enormous! You take pictures and pick up rock samples (pause) just to touch pieces of the moon! (pause) It's time to board the rocket. You leave with a feeling of accomplishment. Lift off. . . . You return to Earth. Crowds on Earth begin cheering. . . . you did it. You were on the moon. (pause) Congratulations (pause) you did it! Think back on your trip, (pause) redream it again and again, (pause) you were on the moon.

To Practice Creative Writing Skills—by a graduate student

1. Have paper and pencil on your desk. Now put your head down on your desk and close your eyes.

   It is the day before Halloween. Pretend you are a pumpkin sitting out in a garden ready to be picked for Halloween. Think about how large you are, what you look like (color, texture), what the weather is like—are you cold, warm, or wet? Do you want to stay in the garden, or be cut up and decorated for Halloween? Are you the only pumpkin in the garden or are there many others?

   Now that you are a pumpkin, put your head up and write down on paper all about yourself.

2. It is Halloween day. Now that you have told me about yourself, put your head down on the desk and close your eyes. I see a young girl coming to the garden and she has picked you for her Halloween party tonight. She brings you into the house and starts to carve your face for she wants you to decorate her party table for tonight. Think about—how do you feel while they are carving—what do you look like now—do you have a sad or a funny face? Do you have a candle burning inside of you? What is the girl saying to you while she is making your face?

   Now put your head up and begin writing and telling me all about your experiences while being made into a Halloween pumpkin.

3. Put your head down on the desk. Close your eyes. You are on the party table and it is Halloween night—the night of the party. You watch the children coming to the party. What are they wearing? Are there many children? How do they like you—do they think you are a funny pumpkin or a sad pumpkin—what are the children doing at the party—playing games, eating? Are you happy at this party or do you wish you were still out in the garden?

   Put your head up and begin writing all about your thoughts, wishes on this night of Halloween as the chosen pumpkin decorating this girl's table.

The use of imagery stimulation is limited only to the teacher's imagination. Following are three primary applications:
   A. As the vehicle for language experience.
   B. As a vehicle of relaxation and suggestion.
   C. As a vehicle for memory improvement.

Lesson 13
January 25, 1980

Today's lesson went very well. Hans is maintaining his new positive outlook to a point that I'm utterly amazed.

We did deep breathing and "Butterfly Fantasy" during the preparation phase. During the active phase I read to Hans from a science experiment book. He chose an experiment he wants us to do together. (Making a miniature fire extinguisher.) We drew up a list of materials we will need. We spent the rest of the active session reviewing old stories and vocabulary.

During the passive phase we worked on word visualization. I also sang words to him in three intonations while he looked on peacefully at flash cards. This type of reinforcement works very well for Hans. We agreed that during our next lesson we would do our science experiment.

Hans is still resisting rhythmic breathing.

Lesson 14
February 1, 1980

Today we went through the typical preparation period with Hans responding very well. During the active phase we did the science experiment and Hans was so excited. But when we came back to my office to write up the experiment Hans lowered his head and refused input. This has not happened since his earlier lessons. I insisted that the experiment be written, so I did it myself with little input from Hans. The following is, as of today, without a title. Hans promises a title later.

> Today we made a small fire extinguisher and some gas. The gas was made out of vinegar and baking soda. We put out a small fire and a match.

When the story was finished, he eagerly read it several times. I feel that this activity reminded him too much of some earlier activity in school that might have caused Hans embarrassment so he experienced a momentary regression.

When he left he reminded me that we have yet to complete his space journey story. I promised him we would. That was his way of saying, "Hey, I really do like to write stories," even though he balked at writing up the experiment.

Lesson 15
February 5, 1980

Hans arrived today his usual cheerful self. Our little episode over the writing up of the experiment was forgotten. It is a very important reminder for me that children should not be held accountable for everything they do. An adult could not live with the levels of accountability that children face on a day-to-day basis.

At Hans's request, we used "Butterfly Fantasy" during the preparation phase. I used it only as a vehicle for relaxation and positive suggestion.

Today we read from his space age book, reread his old stories and reviewed his old and new words.

We started a new game we'll call "Machine Gun." I hold up a word and shout it at Hans very rapidly about a dozen times. Then Hans does the same with another word. The object here is to give Hans as many exposures to a word as possible in as many ways as possible. This all, of course, took place during the active phase.

During the passive phase I directed Hans in word visualization with problem words pulled from his many experience charts.

It is well to note here that reading experts say it takes roughly ten to fifteen exposures to a word before it becomes a sight word. Thus, pure repetition is still of value. But this repetition must take on many faces so as not to bore the child.

Lesson 16
February 8, 1980

Today, after relaxation and positive suggestion during the preparation phase, we reviewed his latest story and problem words from that story. We played "Machine Gun" again to review the many new words Hans has been exposed to. He is doing very well and his visual memory is improving. I have been giving the following suggestion repeatedly during the passive sessions. "I am finding that your memory is continually improving; this must make you very happy."

The passive phase consisted of visualization practice and the singing of words as he sat in a relaxed state and watched the flash cards.

Hans is now beginning to join me in the singing. This activity is simply the process of singing the words in the triad of intonations.

Sometimes I spell them out rhythmically so he grasps the "feeling" of syllabication. I do not teach syllabication directly.

Lesson 17
February 17, 1980

Today, following the preliminaries during the preparation phase, we read together and finished his space book. We created new flash cards consisting of words taken from the space book. We worked on these during the passive phase.

Lesson 18
February 18, 1980

It has been a week since I've seen Hans but we were both pleased with how well he recalled his vocabulary today. I am happy to express my belief that Hans's learning barriers are near extinction.

Today, because of my busy schedule, I had to cut Hans' lesson down to thirty minutes so I moved into the active phase immediately and continued writing his new story about our adventures in outer space. He surprised me by asking for his relaxation time. This pleased me because he is now seeing the value of it. Since he no longer exhibits task avoidance ploys, I'm sure that that was not his motivation for asking.

Hans resists rhythmic breathing during the passive-reinforcement phase. Often, we do deep breathing for a few minutes to set the pace for the peacefulness and calm of this session. I am stepping up word visualization practice since this seems to help him remember words, if not improve his memory in general.

Lesson 19
February 19, 1980

Today's lesson went very well. We are now finished with one chapter of his story, "Adventures in Outer Space."

Lesson 20
February 21, 1980

Sometimes I grope for ideas to liven up the active session. I have found that Hans is full of ideas for activities. So I have stopped groping and ask Hans what he'd like to do next.

I have a set of books on tape so we tried "The Eagle Has Landed." First we read the short story together, then listened to the tape. Hans said he never wanted to do that again. I was glad! That just isn't natural. Listening is a related but different skill than reading. As Frank Smith (98) says, "Often we overload the processing system making it impossible for children to handle all the input." So we'll just stay with reading for now and do listening activities as a separate entity.

Lesson 21
February 25, 1980

Today is another "red letter day." These are the days that give me the encouragement to move on and continue my work. We completed our preparation phase by using "Once Upon a Tree" and were beginning the active phase when Hans said, "Hey, let me do the writing." Thus far I did all the writing, and this is the first time Hans ever showed any interest in writing the original story. He insisted that he would rather use an overhead projector. I was thrilled to hear this request since it was indicative of the fact that he is lowering his defenses. Hans said I could spell words for him if he had problems. Thus, he wrote Chapter 2 of our space story himself.

Lessons 22 Through 25
March 10 Through March 24, 1980

Two weeks had lapsed during which time I did not see Hans due to spring vacation and other conflicts. Rather than write a lesson-by-lesson account I wish to discuss the activities we engaged in so the reader can grasp a variety of activities that are possible during the active phase. The preparation and passive phases do not change appreciably since I have, by now, discovered what works best for Hans in terms of mild calming, positive suggestion, and reinforcement. The following activities were successful for Hans.

The Journal

Each story that is written is typed and put in his journal for rereading and extra practice. He is very proud of this journal. In fact his mother said that he often takes it to bed with him. This book symbolizes success to Hans since he can read everything in it. To broaden the use of the journal, Hans suggested a glossary which lists all of his new words in alphabetical order. This is excellent for him because no words are entered unless they have been permanently assigned to his memory.

Making Use of Strengths and Interests

Hans loves anything to do with outer space and rocketry. His mother purchased a model rocket for him which we put together. The outcome of this experience in academic terms is shown below exactly as it appeared on the experience chart and will now appear in his journal.

Rocket Parts

String	— The *string* is on the parachute.
Lug	— A *lug* is necessary for launching.
Engine	— The *engine* will push the rocket up.
Fins	— The *fins* help the rocket fly.
Engine Holder	— The *engine holder* held the engine up.
Engine Block	— The *engine block* kept the engine from ramming the capsule.
Dummy Engine	— The *dummy engine* didn't know two plus two.
Nose Cone	— The *nose cone* falls off.

Hans has completed his rocket now and will soon build mine for me. We will launch them together and open up a whole new world of vocabulary for us.

SOME AFTERTHOUGHTS

Overhead Projector

As a teacher I never was very high on using the overhead as a teaching tool. But Hans loves it and will "write, write, write" using this simple machine. Perhaps seeing his words, drawings and labels appear large and bold on the wall gives him a special thrill and provides extra impact. That kid is just fantastic! I am learning far more than he is, so I've changed my mind and urge that teachers encourage children to use this simple machine in any way they wish.

Transition to Books

Be sure the child is ready before placing him back into books of any kind. A good way to do it is to select a simple book and acquaint yourself with the vocabulary you feel will be a problem for the student. Prepare the student in advance and he will experience a real lift when he "zooms" through it easily.

Use of Oral Reading

The practice of oral reading has been criticized in the literature and for many valid reasons. This practice however, has some important uses in the intuitive approach since, for example, it is an excellent informal diagnostic tool. The practitioner *never* asks a child with a reading problem to read orally alone, but says, "Read this with me," thus removing the curse of totally humiliating the child. Careful observation of the child during the partner reading exercise will give the teacher information regarding words and sounds the child cannot identify, i.e., hesitation, lip movements, and facial expressions.

Another most important use for oral partner reading is for the sake of reinforcement and repetition of new words in context since multiple exposure is a necessity.

Read exciting stories to the students and allow them to listen passively. Follow this with a language experience lesson. (Summaries, endings, plot changes, etc.) Hans has not arrived at this point yet, since he prefers his own stories.

Word Drills

As many interesting and creative ways of providing multiple exposure to the new words as the practitioner can create are important, i.e., word ladders, word charts, and flash cards taped all over the walls of the teaching area. This provides for spontaneous drill in a traditional fashion or through using the triad of intonation.

It is essential, though, that the word be used in a sentence so as to assure "meaning."

New Name Concept

An important activity which Hans has, thus far, not engaged in is the writing of a new biography for himself, void of all his weaknesses and packed with positive new goals and strengths. This activity should be done by the tenth lesson, but Hans was not ready for it; he preferred to engage in other content.

Summary

It was extremely unfortunate that Hans moved to another city following the last lesson and was unable to continue his reading therapy. Hans had grown considerably in an academic way and even more so in a personal way, but he had not yet achieved total extinction of the barriers that were interfering with his learning and happiness in general. He had begun to develop his own decoding system and felt more comfortable in the reading act, while growing in vocabulary development and comprehension at the same time.

Chapter 11

DIAGNOSIS AND REMEDIATION
OF PSYCHOSOCIAL PROBLEMS

It is generally agreed that psychological and social problems (psychosocial) exist in most problem readers and whether they are a cause or result of the reading problem is not as important as dealing with them. I have been more successful in clinical work by dealing with these problems immediately and concurrently by integrating specific activities into the remedial sessions that face the psychosocial problems head on. As has been illustrated earlier, these psychosocial activities are handled in the preparation phase and integrated into the active and passive phase by becoming the vehicle for what skills are to be learned. This creates a meaningful emotional impact on the student and allows him to work out his problems while at the same time learning new reading skills under disguise. Many authorities from Ekwall (31) to Spache (99) have identified the types of psychosocial problems that most problem readers exhibit.

It is senseless to attempt to formally diagnose the psychosocial problems for the reasons that most of the formal measures are very subjective in interpretation. Besides, most reading specialists are not trained to administer or interpret measures of personality adjustment. Then, too, most problem readers have been tested to death as it is and find more tests to have devastating rather than positive effects.

The activities described in previous chapters are behaviorally oriented and designed to desensitize the student while at the same time provide a stimulus for reading, writing, sharing, and interacting in many ways. They are designed to integrate the child's personality and feelings with actual, but incidental, remediation of language problems. The reader will notice that suggested activities are designed to develop all communication skills, not just reading.

This appears to be sensible since one cannot really separate the language arts, and the excellence of one relies on the other. This process requires total teacher involvement in an authoritative yet understanding way. The process is verbal and nonverbal since behavior, action, and oral and written language are all involved.

By now it is apparent to the reader how these activities are to be sequenced in terms of the three basic phases. Great care must be exercised by the teacher to insure proper preparation. The child must enter the learning situation with an altered state of consciousness. This simply means that instead of fear and anxiety the child exhibits confidence and trust as he or she will in fact learn easily. The preceding chapters have described the procedures to attain this. The teacher, as in any method, is the "key." The active phase possesses the attributes to total involvement and conscious sensory activity. The passive phase is more nonspecific in terms of attention and relies more on the auditory channel and aesthetic qualities inherent in man. The use of music, rhythm, and intonation enhances the pseudopassive state and integration of what is to be learned.

When "R," a seventh grader, was informally checked on the spelling of thirty of the total words he had learned over a five-week period he spelled twenty-nine out of the thirty correctly. This was indeed a great feat for him. Significant here is the fact that he spelled them all in the same rhythm and intonation by which he learned them. This is true of most other students I have worked with. Thus one can conclude that rhythm and intonation does in fact ease learning and facilitate memory. While this sample is small (sixty-four students), thousands of students in other parts of the world are learning various types of subject matter in this way with ease and greater efficiency (37).

Psychodramatic activity is valuable not only in terms of initiating behavioral change but in terms of reinforcement of needed language skills. This activity is appropriate for the active session, but can be put into an added session called the psychodramatic phase. This is especially convenient if it is an activity that is ongoing and will require more than a twenty- to thirty-minute time span. If an activity which is initiated during the preparation, active, and passive phases of a combined hour's duration is deemed necessary, the next one-hour lesson can be of a psychodramatic nature with the above-stated objectives. Ideas for psychodramatic activity will be provided in a later chapter along with suggestions for sequencing this phase.

In severe cases such as Hans's formal diagnosis is not only not necessary but probably impossible. Hans could not decode by the method he was being plagued with. His feelings and emotions were also interfering with even getting a start in reading. His former training was geared toward the child who learned in spite of the method used. In Hans's case each lesson was programmed in the direction of failure and presented as a segmented series of events that supposedly would have led to reading. Reading success could not and would not happen because, for whatever reasons, Hans cannot process as other children do.

Whether Hans is a learning disability case or a reading disability case does not matter. One must simply recognize that in cases like Hans's, the "freedom to compensate" must be permitted to effect a change in reading achievement. This freedom from phonics and other segmented instruction will lead to a personalized decoding process that the teacher may never understand. Instruction must lead to new discoveries about reading and the words that make up reading, while at the same time, integrating the background of experiences and perceptions of personalized reading.

To say that no diagnostic work takes place in the intuitive reading approach is not accurate; it does take place, but it explores different avenues, which lead to a more affective and effective program.

If the key to change is a sudden turnabout in learning expectation of the child, then initial diagnosis is indeed inappropriate, since it is viewed as a negative act by many students and can lower rather than raise learning expectations

This approach demands that both parties involved (teacher and student) start over. The student and the teacher must accept and believe the following assumptions:

A. Everyone can learn to read. (especially this child)
B. What happened in the past is not important because it is the present and the future that count.
C. The periphery of learning barriers that surround the reading problem is the "problem" rather than reading itself.

Thus diagnosis, as it relates directly to reading, is not the correct starting place in many cases because most students have already had all the needed testing anyway. Diagnosis, as Rupley and Blair indicate (86), is an ongoing process. As practitioners work with children, everything they need to know will be observed if they know what to look for.

Since the intuitive approach views acquisition of reading skills as an outcome and not the primary objective, the direction of diagnosis is changed. The following diagnostic information is primary and relates back to the learning barriers discussed earlier: (see anti-suggestive barriers)

    A. How does this child view himself?

    B. How does the client view learning?

    C. What socio-cultural barriers interfere with the child's learning?

    D. How does the child intuitively feel about his ability to learn?

    E. How does he or she rationalize at a conscious level about what reading is and its place in his or her life?

    F. What personality traits interfere with his or her learning?

    G. What habits does the child have that interfere with learning?

    H. What are the daily fears this child has?

    I. What are the client's interests and strengths?

    J. What are the child's goals and immediate needs?

The above are the real concerns that must be dealt with immediately. The prescriptions are affective, the activities reflect what is learned about the child so that reading and writing become the tools to overcome the student's problems with the dual outcome of improved self-image and reading skills.

Table V should help the teacher understand the diagnostic-prescriptive procedure applicable here. The teacher's perception and creativity are key elements if the child is to succeed.

Thus diagnostic and prescriptive activities center on the child and his feelings, emotions, fears, needs, etc., rather than the reading skills directly. This is necessary since the intuitive approach has the primary objective of making reading skills an outcome of activities that have the whole child in the center.

To attempt to diagnose the current word attack skills of a student or group of students is self-defeating. Children with reading and learning problems have already failed at the traditional approaches and it is senseless to continue to build in more failure. To chart students' deficits leads only to deficit teaching and a fragmented program. The holistic approach, which views the child, reading, and the reading act in an integrated way, leads to the development of the personalized decoding system and allows the

TABLE V
SUGGESTED DIAGNOSTIC AND REMEDIAL TECHNIQUES

Diagnostic Consideration	How Discovered	Remedial Techniques	Reading Outcomes
A. How does the child feel?	A. Observation B. Interview parents, teachers, and counselors C. Oral attitude inventory D. Do Self-Portrait	A. Do Self-Portrait (written with teacher help) B. Direct suggestions of positive nature C. Indirect suggestion, drill with words on flash cards taken from self-portrait (positives)	A. Key-personal vocabulary development B. Basic sight words C. Attitude that reading is personalized D. Develop personalized decoding system
B. How does the client view learning?	A. Discussion with child B. Observation, what and how does the child learn best? C. Do: Early Pleasant Learning Recall (EPLR)	A. Make group of flash cards reflecting feelings. B. Do follow-up on EPLR. Compare pleasant learning experience with unpleasant by doing an experience chart.	A. Situational vocabulary development. B. Basic sight vocabulary C. Personalized Decoding System.
C. What sociocultural barriers interfere with learning?	A. Survey and observation: 1. What type of achievement is important in that locale? 2. What "no no's" does the child live with (value system)? 3. Is success, goal setting, and reading important in that culture?	A. Write experience charts covering now and the future. Set new goals if necessary. B. Direct positive suggestion regarding self-worth and future needs. C. Hero worship activities	A. Situational and futuristic vocabulary as personalized by the child. (i.e., in the future I will be strong, positive, self-assured. These words must be part of the child's vocabulary before it will be part of him.)
D. How does the child intuitively feel about his ability to learn?	A. Observation of behavior in pleasant and unpleasant situations that are spontaneous.	A. Direct suggestion during preparation and passive phases. B. Create success situations during active sessions.	A. Attitude reformation about reading and learning. "In writing."

TABLE V (Continued)

SUGGESTED DIAGNOSTIC AND REMEDIAL TECHNIQUES

Diagnostic Consideration	How Discovered	Remedial Techniques	Reading Outcomes
E. How does the student rationalize at a conscious level (What reading is and its place in life.)	A. Observation B. Discussion C. Through lesson evaluations D. Surveys: attitude, interest, etc.	A. Experience charts —Reading is . . .) B. Be a good model C. Experience chart: Reading is important because . . . D. Experience chart, I feel reading is important (not important) because . . . E. Discuss value and place of reading in society F. Positive suggestion	A. Builds vocabulary related to the child's philosophy of reading. B. Personalized decoding system.
F. What personality traits interfere with the student's learning?	A. Observation B. Discussion C. Survey questions D. Self-Portraits	A. Imagery activity centered around improving attitudes about learning B. Motivation and positive suggestion C. New name activity (previously discussed) D. Give child insights into himself as it relates to learning.	A. Enhancing visualization skills B. Developing positive views about the reading and learning act. C. Personal emotion-packed vocabulary D. Developing a personalized decoding system
G. What personality traits interfere with learning?	A. Discussion B. Observation and social and academic situations	A. Self-portraits B. Word stimulation games (i.e., In a group you feel, at home you wish, your friends make you feel, reading is, learning is, etc.) C. Positive suggestion as it relates to personal strengths and affecting changes in weak areas. D. EPLR activities	A. Key word vocabulary development. B. Enhance creative writing abilities. C. Enhance oral expression. D. Basic sight word. E. Personalized decoding system.

TABLE V (Continued)
SUGGESTED DIAGNOSTIC AND REMEDIAL TECHNIQUES

Diagnostic Consideration	How Discovered	Remedial Techniques	Reading Outcomes
		E. Write: "The New Me."	
H., I., J. What fears, habits, goals, needs, strengths, and weaknesses does the student have?	A. Orally given interest and attitude inventories B. Observation C. Discussion with student, teachers, and parents D. Experience charts.	A. Word stimulation games. B. Experience stories. C. Time management activities. D. Goal setting activities E. Role playing F. Experience chart G. Acting out situation using puppets	A. Key personal vocabulary B. Oral fluency C. Creating writing D. Orally reading fluency expression E. Basic sight words F. Personalized decoding system.

humans infinite power of "compensation" to operate.

It is interesting here to mention that so many adults who had reading problems as children will state that it was not until they were in seventh or eighth grade that they began to improve in their reading skills. This has been attributed to maturation by most educators, but the writer feels that it is not maturation at all. A number of researchers believe that facility in learning language skills diminishes as the child progresses through the grades (108). It could well be that as a student reaches junior high levels where there is less formal reading instruction and more focus on content, students for the first time experience a "new freedom" that allows this compensation to take place.

WHO CAN BENEFIT

This approach can be used for students who have the misfortune of carrying around a number of labels. It is effective for the so-called learning disabled, reading disabled, and even emotionally disturbed children (70).

The approach has been successful not only as a remedial technique but as a way of accelerating learning in foreign languages (92), mathematics (79), and other curriculum areas.

Teachers should not feel that the intuitive approach can be effective only one-on-one. It is better to go "one-on-one" in severe cases, but it is also effective in larger corrective groupings in the regular classroom setting. One must use and gain experience using the techniques to discover the power and numerous applications it has. Try, for example, the white cloud exercise with an entire class. Take them into the cloud and travel with them to distant, interesting places. Have the students relax with eyes closed while you describe what they are seeing. It stimulates the very foundations of the child's imagination and provides him the freedom to feel and think. Allow each student the opportunity to see what he wants to see. There is nothing far out about this exercise — it is simply a good creative writing project. Once the trip has ended and students are asked to open their eyes and sit up straight, the preparation phase is complete. The active phase would follow as students write about their experiences. To complete the suggestopaedic sequence, the teacher can follow up with an activity for the passive phase. One way to do it would be to walk around and look at students' papers and jot down words they are misspelling on flash cards. When the students finish writing ask them to sit back and relax. Ask them to look at a word on the flash card, then close their eyes and visualize the word while you spell it out in the triad (triad is discussed earlier). Music can be used to make it an enjoyable and creative event.

SUMMARY

Diagnosis is affective in nature. The teacher wishes to discover feelings, fears, habits, interests, strengths, and weaknesses. Activities are designed to discover affective needs followed by activities which will give the student insights and an opportunity to express these orally and/or in writing. These activities are to be non-threatening and holistic in nature, allowing the student to enhance his general language development, develop a personalized decoding system by way of compensation, and grow personally through self-discovery.

This intuitive approach subscribes to the general principles of suggestopaedia and can be used in remedial as well as classroom corrective. It can be used one on one in severe cases or in small groups for nearly any purpose, including accelerated learning in any curriculum area. For more information see Schuster (93), Bancroft (7), Prichard (79), and Ostrander and Schroeder (73).

Chapter 12

EXTENDED USE OF
IMAGERY AND LANGUAGE EXPERIENCE

T he previous chapters outlined the preparation and active and passive sessions and provided some concise examples using this three-phase structure. This chapter will be used to provide more imagery ideas and broaden the reader's concept of structuring the teaching session keeping in mind the necessary sequences. The lesson example that follows uses the same basic sequence but puts drama into a session called the psychodramatic session instead of its use in the active session. Table III, model C, illustrates this sequence along with some time suggestions. The time allotment for each phase can vary according to needs at the time. It is possible, by this time, that practice has shortened the preparation phase to about five minutes. The reader should by now be able to create his or her own ideas keeping in mind the important sequence and components of the intuitive approach. The example to follow will suggest other possible activities to increase use of imagery and language experience as well as drama.

Another Lesson Example

The *Edmund Fitzgerald*, a large ore boat that sank in Lake Superior on November 10, 1976, will provide the background for this complete lesson example. It illustrates that any topic from current events to the child's own personal experiences can be combined with imagery, suggestion, language experience, and creative dramatics to produce a powerful experience the child will not easily forget. When creating these experiences a carefully thought-out plan must be written to assure the smooth delivery that is necessary.

The objectives should be carefully thought out and stated, but it is obvious by now that many overall objectives are consistent with

111

each lesson and need not be rewritten each time. These overall objectives are listed here and should be remembered when writing more specific daily objectives.

Overall objectives:
    A. To provide a quality learning experience.
    B. To provide a relaxed and positive learning atmosphere.
    C. To provide a vehicle to raise self-concept, positive attitudes about learning, and new learning expectations.
    D. To provide a vehicle to establish conscious-unconscious state of rapport. (A comfortable state of awareness.)
    E. To establish hypersuggestibility.
    F. To teach needed language skills.
    G. To provide for imagery development.
    H. To provide for positive suggestion.

Specific objectives:
    A. To provide practice in imagery.
    B. To develop writing skills.
    C. To develop an enriched oral, reading, and writing vocabulary.
    D. To gain insights into the word recognition skills.
    E. To provide interaction activity.
    F. To develop creative dramatic insights.

Preparation Phase:

Step 1   Suggest relaxation.

Step 2   Establish conscious-unconscious rapport (use deep breathing or E.P.L.R. and suggest easy learning).

Step 3   Develop deeper relaxation and imagery. (The following white cloud exercise will provide the needed imagery practice and the content for the active phase.) It goes as follows:

Imagine that you are lying on your back on the grass on a warm summer day, and that you are watching the clear blue sky without a single cloud in it (pause). You are lying there very comfortably, very relaxed, quite happy with yourself (pause). You simply are enjoying the beauty of watching the clear, beautiful, blue sky (pause). As you are lying there completely relaxed, enjoying yourself (pause) way off on the horizon you note a tiny white cloud (pause). You are fascinated by the simple beauty of the small white cloud against the clear blue sky background (pause). The little white cloud starts to move slowly towards you (pause). You are lying there completely relaxed, very much at peace with yourself, watching the little white cloud drift slowly toward you (pause). The little white cloud drifts slowly toward you (pause). Completely relaxed and at peace with yourself, you watch the little white cloud slowly come toward you (pause). You are enjoying the beauty of the clear blue sky and the tiny white cloud (pause). Finally the little white cloud comes to a stop overhead (pause). Completely relaxed, you are enjoying this beautiful scene (pause). You are very relaxed, very much at home with yourself, and simply enjoying the beauty of the little white cloud in the blue sky (pause). Now become the little white cloud. Project yourself into it (pause). You are the little white cloud, completely diffused, puffy, relaxed, very much at home with yourself (pause). Now you are completely relaxed, your mind is completely calm (pause), you are pleasantly relaxed, ready to proceed with the trip. (Proceed with a trip over a zoo, foreign country, etc.) (Schuster, Bordon and Gritton, 93, p. 26.)

The child is now part of the cloud free to go where it goes. (Suggest that he will learn new skills today very easily because he is free.)

Teacher: "We are floating over Lake Superior. You are safe and comfortable (pause). But looking down you see that a storm is brewing and the waves look like giants sitting down and then standing up. The wind must be strong and cold. Yet you are not part of that wind and cold. You see a large ship. It is slender and long and entering the heart of the storm (pause). How you wish you could help because the ship is being thrown around like a small and helpless cork. (Do you see it?) Suddenly a large wave forms in front of the ship and another fierce looking wave forms in the rear (pause). The ship is raised out of the water, you hear a tremendous "clap" (listen) like angry thunder and it is all over. What did you see happening (pause)? Where is the ship?"

The children are now hypersuggestive and stimulated. What happened? (Pause long enough to develop the scene mentally.) Suggest that they are now floating back to land and have returned to their original position before they entered the cloud. Ask them to open their eyes.

Active phase:

A. Read the ballad of the "Wreck of the *Edmund Fitzgerald*" to the students. Allow them to formulate their own ideas of why the ship sank. Did it capsize, or did it break in half? Make these suggestions before the students write but encourage their own theories. (A recording of this ballad is available for added stimulus.)

B. Have children write a story about their trip, their feelings, impressions, and conclusions.

C. Have students share their stories orally.

D. Collect the papers and allow the students to relax and visit while you correct the papers and make corrections for them. Use these errors and other key words (of emotional nature) to make a quick set of flash cards. Jot down the first name of the child whom the word belongs to on the back of the card for your record. Then return the papers to the owners.

E. Have the students rewrite the experience as they recorded it, along with the proper corrections, into their experience journal.

While the student does this the teacher gets the music ready and prepares for the passive session and the remainder of the active session. Put the cards in some sensible order so a story will evolve in a spontaneous manner.

The following are two actual products that evolved out of this lesson. Read these carefully so as to discover the key words, the errors, and phonic problems that emerged. These must all be carefully incorporated into the passive phase of the lesson.

Example A*: Eighth Grade Boy

I saw a Big bunch of men jumping off the ship I saw huge waves in front and behind the ship. I saw a big bunch of rain and wind clouds over the ship. I saw a big flouting cyclone suckin up the sailors that jumped of the ship. I saw the hills of the Duluth side sink in the sea as I followed them along the shore line.

Example B: Seventh Grade Boy

I saw pink and yellow round squish things that muntched together and a ship frunt and ping and yellow and a holl in the botom sane and heard a

---

*Both of the boys involved in these examples are labeled as dyslexic children as a result of neurological and other examinations prior to coming to the center.

lot of noise and the boat going to the bottom and fish and sea coral and rocks and moor fish.

F. The final portion of the active phase involves both auditory and visual activity with key words and problem words. In this lesson, these words were presented to the students visually (flash cards) and auditorily (spelling words orally). This should be followed by mental imagery practice: Students are asked to close their eyes and see the words as the teacher spells them slowly syllable by syllable.

Word integration does not appear to happen automatically and instantaneously with the problem readers. Thus practice with mental visualization is very important and requires extended use in the intuitive lessons. It is well known in the reading field that problem readers have poor visual imagery skills (79) and the use of imagery trips enhances this development. That, coupled with close correlation of content from the preparation phase on to the passive phase provides continuity, deeper meaning and maintenance of a relaxed, suggestive learning atmosphere.

Passive phase:

A. Students are asked to relax in their lounge chairs and attend to their breathing for a few minutes.

B. The teacher provides positive suggestions regarding what will happen during the passive session.

The teacher's mood, expression, and generally positive nonverbal behavior is strong indirect suggestion. She must act as if she believes what she is suggesting. Suggestions such as the following are appropriate:

1. You will learn and remember the spellings and meanings of these words easily.
2. This session is fun and relaxing.
3. Pretend you are at a concert or a play.
4. You will come away from this activity feeling good and enriched.
5. You are all excellent learners.

The following dialogue is based on the two example writing experiences presented earlier. It is presented by the teacher with intonation and varied rhythm which becomes a moving experience when combined with background music. Remember the simple triad that is to be used: Normal voice (N.V.), whisper (Wh.), and loud voice (L.). The teacher may attempt to keep time with the music or vary the rhythm any way she wishes through syllabication.

N.V.: "A bunch of men were jumping overboard."
Wh.: "Bunch—"B-U-N-CH"
L.: "The sky looked pink and yellow."
N.V.: "Yellow—"YE-LL-O-W"
Wh.: "We saw a floating cyclone."
L.: "Floating—"FL-OAT-ING"
N.V.: "FL-OAT-ING"
Wh.: "FL-OAT-OAT-OAT-ING""*
L.: "There was a hole in the bottom of the ship."
N.V.: "Hole—"H-O-L-E"
Wh.: "Bottom-bottom"
L.: "BO-TT-OM"
N.V.: "BO-TT-OM"
Wh.: "BO-TT-OM"
L.: Etc. (Using all problem and key emotional words.)

This dramatic presentation is highly effective. It takes only several repeats for real problem words to sink in. It is often helpful if students keep their eyes closed and visually image the syllables dancing about inside their heads. The rhythm, as the reader will notice, carries the syllabication and phonic elements.

PSYCHODRAMATIC SESSION: This lesson included a psychodramatic session while the other lesson examples did not. If the teacher wishes to engage in a prolonged dramatic experience it is best to pull the drama out of the active session and add this dramatic portion.

In this lesson students wrote a skit for a shadow show depicting the tragic sinking of the *Edmund Fitzgerald*. This skit provides a language experience that is totally stimulating and requires that extensive imagery takes place so that props, characters, and entire scenes are from imagination alone.

---

*The word floating was repeated in a number of ways since one of the boys has a problem with words containing vowel digraphs. (This practice has helped him greatly.)

LANGUAGE EXPERIENCE AND INTUITIVE LEARNING

The use of language experience certainly is not new to the American educator and has a strong rationale long recognized in the field of reading. The following exerpts from the classic text by Lee and Allen describe the rationale in excellent detail and give added support to the intuitive approach.

1. *What a child thinks about he can talk about.*
   Teachers begin with the thoughts of each child as the basic ingredient for developing reading skills.
2. *What he can talk about can be expressed in painting, writing, or some other form (as drama).*
   This causes the teacher to realize that to some degree all normal children can already write and read. It cancels out any preconceived notion that a child must have a reading vocabulary of a certain size before he begins to write.
3. *Anything he writes can be read.*
   Experiences with both picture writing and with writing with the etters of our alphabet help the child to recognize hat one is uch more precise than the other and gives the eader more pecific clues about the thinking of the author.
4. *He can read what he writes and what other people write.*
   The child experiences the thrill of reading what other people have written after he has experienced the thrill of seeing his own oral language take a form that can be reproduced by the process called reading.
5. *As he represents his speech sounds with symbols, he uses the same symbols (letters) over and over.*
   Teaching the child to symbolize his speech sounds rather than trying to get him to assign a sound or sounds to a symbol is to take the experience approach to teaching the phonetic elements of our own language.
6. *Each letter in the alphabet stands for one or more sounds that he makes when he talks.*
   At first the teacher records the oral language of the individual to develop this understanding. As the child writes on his own, this understanding matures to the point of including the many variations inherent in the English language.

7. *Every word begins with a sound that he can write down.*
   Understanding how to symbolize initial sounds in words is a breakthrough to the magic realm of reading and writing.
8. *Most words have an ending sound.*
   This, like the understanding above, is a normal development for children who observe speech take the form of writing.
9. *Many words have something in between.*
   This is an understanding that offers a long-range teaching program. It continues to be a fascinating part of learning throughout the life of the individual.
10. *Some words are used over and over in our language and some words are not used very often.*
    Vocabulary control is built into the language of the individual. A few words are used hundreds of times, others only rarely.
11. *What he has to say and write is as important to him as what other people have written for him to read.*
    Many teachers have difficulty with the implementation of this understanding. However, a teacher who cannot demonstrate a real thrill over the output of ideas in his own classroom leaves out one of the principal ingredients of the formula.
12. *Most of the words he uses are the same ones which are used by other people who write for him to read.*
    Helping the child to get a built-in feeling that the main purpose of reading is to deal with the ideas of the author rather than the words he uses is a strength of the method. In effect, they read from the beginning as though they were carrying on a conversation with the author. Because they know that the story will be written in words which they use in their own speech and writing, children are released from the fear that they may not be able to read it. They are well on the way to independence in reading skills at a much earlier age than it was formerly thought possible. (Lee and Allen, 56, pp. 5–9)

The use of language experience approach in remedial reading serves the practitioner in a number of ways as mentioned above. In the intuitive approach where one views reading holistically and the child as a total person with interacting cognitive, affective, and psychomotor domains, other ends can be met by integrating that approach with suggestion and imagery. Language experience, in fact, is an outcome of imagery and suggestion when there is proper integration of the lesson sequences. With the use of imagery and suggestion integrated into the lesson the child can be reached not only in terms of his reading problems, but in terms of his attitude and self-concept problems. Table VI illustrates activities that can be used to approach specific problems. These activities can be applied to the intuitive lesson sequence as previously described. These suggested activities are being used successfully in many parts of the world with great success. Chapter 14 will provide some empirical data for the reader that will support some of those procedures.

Summary

Use of psychodrama provides the opportunity for extended use of imagery and language experience by way of play writing, creating props for plays, and writing character sketches.

An example of the use of current events and their application to the intuitive reading approach was given in complete sequence (the sinking of the *Edmund Fitzgerald* in Lake Superior). Many events, local and national, can be used to create stimulating lessons that will provide for extended use of language experience and imagery development.

There is a strong rationale for use of language experience in the teaching of reading both in development and remedial programs. The basic concept is that what can be experienced can be talked about, written, and read. The use of oral language the student already knows is more easily recognized and remembered when seen in printed form.

Imagery and language experience can provide a useful vehicle for reaching affective objectives and reading outcomes, if careful planning and sequencing of events take place.

TABLE VI
SUGGESTED IMAGERY ACTIVITIES

Imagery and Other Activities	Objectives	Teacher Suggestion
1. Have students imagine themselves being their favorite hero (experience the person wholly).	A. Change self-image. B. Raise learning expectations. C. Create positive learning attitudes. D. Provide for language experience, incidental word attack, vocabulary development — other skills according to student needs.	A. You are as good as this favorite person of yours. B. You can do anything you put your mind to. C. He does everything easily, so can you. (The teacher must behave in such a way as to show students he or she really means it.)
2. Early Pleasant Learning Recall (See earlier instructions.)	A. To develop positive attitudes about learning B. To raise learning expectations. C. Develop needed reading skills.	A. Learning is fun and easy. B. Relaxation engages your automatic learning devices and improves memory.
3. Hot air balloon trip. (See instruction detailed earlier.) *Note:* Taking imagery trips has countless possibilities as indicated by the objectives. The trips can also involve vehicles such as: white cloud, mountain top, flying saucer, magic carpet, hang glider, large bird, etc. The student can go anywhere he wishes, experience what he wishes with the teacher's help.	A. Provide for deeper relaxation and vivid imagery. B. Provide a vehicle for language experience. C. Provide feelings of freedom from inhibition. D. Provide for content of lesson. E. Provide for concept development. F. Provide for remediation of word difficulties through follow-up activity.	A. You will enjoy this trip and see many things. B. You will learn many new words and how to spell them. C. You will feel freer than ever before. D. You can write whatever you feel. E. You will learn and remember new words and reading skills.
4. New games and biography. Lozanov suggests this practice at the onset of corrective classes.	A. Reduce fear of making errors. B. Reduce avoidance techniques on the part of students. C. Develop new self-concepts. D. Develop positive learning attitudes.	A. Read about the new you. B. He is everything you want to be and can be. Note: The new biography is very carefully written by the teacher to fit the needs of the student in relation to his psychological setup.

TABLE VI (Continued)
SUGGESTED IMAGERY ACTIVITIES

Imagery and Other Activities	Objectives	Teacher Suggestion
	E. Raise learning expectations.	
5. Word visualization. Take time for the student to mentally see problem words.	A. To allow time for the student to integrate the spelling of a new word along with its meaning.	A. See the whole word. B. See the syllables. C. See the whole word again. D. You'll remember the word. Note: Do this with the Dolch words during an active and passive session.
6. Read short but interesting stories to children. Have students vividly imagine characters, action and endings. Have students reconstruct portions of the story. Stories should reflect interests and emotional needs. Children should always share feelings and ideas. (Stories should be dramatic and exciting with both tragic and happy endings.)	A. Create interest and emotional need for reading. B. Provide character identification. C. To provide for emotional outlet. D. To develop group unity and acceptance. E. To develop appreciation for reading as an emotional experience. F. Provide a vehicle for vocabulary development.	A. This story is exciting. B. You will learn about life as it is (or isn't). C. You will enjoy doing something together, you're all equal, yet different. D. You will see and appreciate the excitement of the story. E. You will want to read stories like this.
7. Vividly imagine an emotional experience. It might be happy, sad, exciting or nerve racking. Write about the experience and share it with peers. Note: This should be a series of lessons. Writing happy, then sad stories followed by other stories of varied emotional tones.	A. Provide the student an opportunity to express his emotions and share with others. B. Provide new insights into self. C. Provide for group belonging. D. Provide a stimulus for language experience. E. Provide a vehicle for vocabulary development. F. Reduce hostility toward those who have hurt them.	A. We've all had good and bad experiences. B. We are all more alike than different. C. By sharing we can help each other. D. We can learn from each other.

TABLE VI (Continued)
SUGGESTED IMAGERY ACTIVITIES

Imagery and Other Activities	Objectives	Teacher Suggestion
8. Situational activity whereby the group solves specific problems as a team. Example: You are all members of a fire department. A young boy crawled to the top of a large tree. Together you must plan a way to get him down. First write your individual plan, then get together and come up with a written master plan. Note: These activities should be reported using police department problems, medical teams, etc.	A. To provide for group interaction, acceptance and cooperation. B. To provide a stimulus for language experience. C. Provide content for remedial instruction. D. Provide stimulus for reading. E. Reduce avoidance and withdrawal tendencies. F. Develop ease in writing ideas down on paper.	A. By putting your ideas together you can solve problems. B. You can learn new ideas and words from each other. C. Everyone's ideas are worthy. D. Any idea can easily be written down.

Chapter 13

PUPPETRY AND PSYCHODRAMA

Drama, as discussed earlier, has been long recognized as a valuable activity in education in all areas of the curriculum (101). Psychodrama involves "drama" in a very special way, since it facilitates the intuitive learning mode and is behaviorally oriented. It is not only valuable as a bearer of the content to be learned but as a vehicle by which the student can act out his feelings at the same time. It appeals to the deep "inners" of man and in the learning environment appears to relax defenses, unite the learning community and set the pace for exciting, natural assimilation of knowledge. Most importantly, it is fun for all involved.

Since many students are not accustomed to its use in the learning-teaching environment, it must be developed gradually in a nonthreatening way. At the beginning it should be nonverbal starting with simple group exercises during the preparation period. Simple, spontaneous body movements directed by the teacher to soothing music is also a good beginning. Simple dances can follow and lead up to the group moving together in unison. Once students are accustomed to simple group activity that imitates beginning drama, the verbal aspects should be introduced. Simple songs and choral reading are good methods because no one has to carry the burden alone. These become vehicles of developing better self-concepts, incidental vocabulary development, and many other benefits commensurate with the intuitive approach.

Puppetry is an excellent way to get students involved concurrently in all the language arts. It is also an excellent way to help students to begin to carry their own parts and develop the self-confidence to act out parts of plays and skits singly rather than as just one more voice in a group.

The purpose of this chapter is to present ideas that are practical and valuable to the teacher that will enrich the total child and his total language development. These activities can take place in the active session or be placed into a phase to follow the passive session. Suggestions as to the implementation of these activities into the proper lesson sequence will be presented at the end of this chapter. This chapter discusses puppetry as the primary drama mode, but is not meant to demean the importance of other types of drama in the intuitive approach.

PSYCHODRAMATIC ACTIVITY: PUPPETRY

Box Puppet

Objective: To provide opportunity for oral language expression.

Materials: The child decorates a small cereal box with a small opening in it to serve as a mouth, pipe cleaner is glued to the back of the mouth so the child can open or close the mouth with his hand from the inside as he manipulates it.

Activity: Child expresses how the puppet looks and feels. Groups can also put on plays with several characters.

Sock Puppet

Objective: To provide the child an opportunity for oral expression.

Materials: The child uses a sock of any color with buttons as eyes and felt as a tongue. Be sure that the sock fits snuggly. (Yarn and other materials can be used to provide hair and other decor.)

Activity: The possibilities are unlimited. Sock puppets are easily constructed to represent numerous animals and people. The child can act out feelings or read stories using the puppet, and groups can perform following the writing of skits. The teacher should often write skits, as well, for students to perform. This provides a way for the teacher to assist students in acting out personal problems.

Shadow Puppet

Objective: To provide the child the opportunity for oral expression and creative writing.

Materials: Lightweight cardboard is used to cut out desired character. A stick is glued to the back to provide for manipulation. The puppets should be decorated with crayon or watercolor and three-dimensionalized with yarn and other materials.

Activity: The opportunities are limitless since puppets are easy and quick to make. Children can use them directly in front of an audience or behind a sheet with a light from the rear to cast a shadow on the sheet. Children, with the teacher's assistance, can write and act out skits which evolved out of the imagery experiences from earlier lessons. In this way the teacher can integrate psychodramatic activity with the rest of the remedial lessons and the skits become more personalized.

Coat Hanger Puppet

Objective: The student will be provided with the opportunity to develop creative expression and develop oral and written language.

Materials: Student(s) will use an ordinary coat hanger and force it into a silk or nylon stocking with the hanger hook straightened out and protruding out of the stocking. The hook hanger is used to manipulate the puppet. A variety of materials can be used to create the desired facial characteristics. (Be it human or animal.)

Activity: Students in ordinary classrooms can get together in groups to write skits and act them out. In the remedial-intuitive session, students' skits will usually evolve out of the imagery activity and must have strong teacher input. It is also suggested that the teacher read fairy tales to the students and that skits evolve out of that activity.

Special Notes to the Teacher:

The teacher plays a very active role when engaging in psychodrama in the intuitive approach. Since children, and especially the remedial students, are often shy about performing, the teacher must serve as a model for children to imitate. Total involvement by the teacher is required from the making of a puppet to assuming a character and actually performing with students. The teacher must become aware of the emotional needs of the student(s) and direct the student into dramatic activity with the following purposes:

A. Act out personal problems and frustrations.

B. To assist the child in reducing learning inhibitions.

C. The teacher can use puppets as a vehicle for providing language development.

D. Creating skits will improve writing skill as well as oral language.

E. To provide the teacher with an opportunity to train students in dramatic expression. (Not only in puppetry but in any type of drama.)

F. Drama provides another vehicle which will insure the maintenance of an intuitive-suggestive atmosphere.

G. Drama also serves as a vehicle for continuing diagnosis. The teacher should listen carefully and record feelings, behavior, and other observations for future corrective activity.

There are as many types of puppets as there are teachers and students making them. The important idea is not what type of puppet (as long as it is functional) but the purpose for which it is used.

The above overall objectives will always be kept in mind when engaging in drama of any kind. The following lists of uses and objectives are more specific. Activities need not have affective objectives to provide affective outcomes, since there is always personal involvement using a puppet and skit written around a child's personal experience. This again points to the necessity of integrating drama with what transpires in the active and passive sessions, at least in theme. Nevertheless drama activities can have the objective of *reinforcement* only. Thus the child is involved in using words, ideas, and feelings he has already experienced in former lessons, making the integration less direct but still effective.

Other content borrowed from the social studies and science curriculum can be used with enhanced motivation for the child more interested in those areas. Yet the outcomes are the same as far as language development is concerned.

The following list of other uses and objectives for puppetry and other forms of drama is certainly not exhaustive but will broaden the perspective for its usage in the intuitive approach.

Affective Uses:

- Act out fears, hostilities, and other problems.
- Act out difficult social situations.
- Act out happy and sad feelings.
- Develop self-confidence and sense of achievement.
- Use to reinforce positive feelings.
- Use to act out Early Pleasant Learning situations. (See E.P.L.R.)
- Develop creative expression.
- Develop a better self-awareness and self-image.
- Provide for discussions of individuality.
- Use puppets to discuss a new self-portrait. (See new name concept.)
- Continued diagnosis.

Language Arts Usage:

- Act out stories read to children.
- Act out imagery experiences children have already engaged in.
- Use skits to review vocabulary already learned.
- Improve listening skills.
- Improve oral expression.
- Improve writing and reading skills.
- Learn to appreciate language in all of its forms.
- Use puppets to teach songs for vocabulary development.
- Use puppets to spell out words in the triad of intonation. (Use a music background.)

Science Curriculum:

- Make puppets of sea animals to learn about them and their habits.
- Use of snowman puppets to discuss climate and weather. Each season can be represented by a puppet to discuss and write about season changes.
- Make puppets of various animals (sock) and discuss the animal's habits. Act out habits, movements, sounds, and other behaviors.

Social Studies Curriculum:

- Act out community helpers showing the roles of various workers.
- Use stick puppets to portray important persons in U.S. history. Children tell about the person they apparently identify with.
- Use pop up puppets to discuss a succession of important events. (Stick puppets are used by a number of children from behind a table. Each puppet pops up at the right time.)

Suggested Implementation

It would be redundant to repeat the objectives for the above-suggested activities since it is obvious that these can be used either as a follow-up to some other language experience or as stimulus for a language experience. In either case, the outcomes would be the further development of listening, speaking, reading, and writing skills. Activities of this nature provide the content for teaching vocabulary and word recognition skills in an incidental way. Not only is the child's language enriched but so is the child.

These activities are also diagnostic in nature since the alert teacher will perceive specific academic and affective needs of the student. Many activities for the active and passive sessions will evolve out of those episodes since written and oral vocabulary need can be assessed in the process. This will be illustrated in Table VII.

Students need not always use puppets in the psychodramatic session. The same ideas can be applied without the use of puppets. Other types of psychodrama are encouraged: Pantomime, role playing, plays and skits without puppets, choral reading, operettas, and actual community-centered activities.

It is probably not necessary to discuss the various forms of dramatics here since experienced teachers are at least aware of its use. But community-centered activity should be touched upon briefly.

This concept is likened to a field trip but oriented more toward language development and attitude formation.

TABLE VII

SEQUENCING THE PSYCHODRAMATIC PHASE

Class Period (1 Hr) Phase Sequence A	Class Period (1 Hr) Phase Sequence B	Notes
1. *Psychodramatic* Children have written a skit about favorite fairy tales, made puppets, and acted out the skits to peers. *Teacher* Records problem words from written skits and notes word recognition problems along with behaviorally oriented problems. 2. *Preparation* Use of three-step preparation. *Active Phase* Teacher presents on flash cards key and problem words, engages in incidental teaching of word recognition problems taken from psychodramatic session. *Passive* Use of music, rhyme, intonation, and pseudo-passivity to reinforce the vocabulary learned.	1. *Preparation* Use of three step preparation—(include E.P.L.R.) *Active* Students relate orally and in writing their early pleasant learning experience. *Teacher* Records problem words and key words along with word recognition problems she perceives from writings. *Passive* Usual use of music, rhyme, intonation, and pseudopassivity to reinforce the vocabulary learned. 2. *Psychodramatic* Students act out with or without puppets their early pleasant learning experience.	A. In Phase Sequence A the psychodramatic episode served as the stimulus for what happened during the next lesson which involved the usual three phases. B. In Phase Sequence B the three phase lesson stimulated the psychodramatic episode. C. Notice the assessment is ongoing and is always followed by a passive skill reinforcement session. Thus there is some flexibility in the use of psychodrama as far as sequencing goes.

Examples:

1. Have children interview prominent community leaders and report back to the group orally and in writing.
2. Have children volunteer for community services. (Clean a park or mow a lawn for an elderly person and report back to the group.)
3. Have children observe adults doing a specific task and report back in descriptive terms. (Painter, bricklayer, etc.)

Summary

In the final analysis students must begin to view themselves as worthy people capable of doing whatever they set their minds to do. Learning language skills is an intuitive or incidental outcome of a pleasant and worthwhile experience.

Psychodrama takes on many forms and is either a stimulus for a writing-reading experience or the outcome of that. (See Appendix for in-depth puppetry ideas and plans.)

Chapter 14

PERTINENT RESEARCH DATA

The purpose of this chapter is to present to the interested reader some empirical information regarding components and practices of the suggestological approach (*intuitive* as this author calls it). It is not the purpose of this chapter to provide a complete review since the primary focus of the research in this text has been to equate the components of suggestopaedia with what already has been recognized in western education. Nevertheless, some studies that relate to the intuitive approach will be discussed briefly.

SALT

A society to study Lozanov style suggestopaedia was instituted in August of 1975 under the name Suggestive-Accelerative Learning and Teaching (SALT). The first President of SALT was Dr. Donald Schuster, Ph.D. of Iowa State University, Ames, Iowa. Other founders are as follows: Ray Benitez-Bordon, associated with the University of Iowa, Iowa City, Iowa; Charles Gritton, from Des Moines Public Schools, Des Moines, Iowa; and Dr. Dean Held, Assistant Professor of Teacher Education of the University of Wisconsin-Superior. The organization has grown considerably since then, with members from many states and nations contributing to annual symposiums and a research journal.

The purpose for the SALT society is to experiment with the Lozanov methodology and make available data and information to promote effective teaching. At this time more information is available regarding the use of this suggestological-intuitive approach as it relates to experiments in the teaching of foreign languages than remedial reading and learning disability per se. Some of these experiments will be discussed along with what is available in the field of remedial reading at this time.

RESEARCH STUDIES RELATED TO SUGGESTOPAEDIA

In a research project reported by Dr. Donald Schuster of Iowa State University (92), Spanish students in the Lozanov experimental sections learned the content of the beginning Spanish course in approximately half the time as did the regular class sections receiving traditional lessons. While the students learned the content in half the class time, they did insignificantly poorer on final exams. Thus, the results appear to be both encouraging and somewhat discouraging. It is interesting to note that the experimental section did slightly better on the spoken lab final.

Lozanov (62) remains somewhat vague and reports his results in percentages and volume learned. Little data is available from his works directly and he reports only that students could learn a foreign language from five to fifty times faster. He also reports that in four alternating half days students could learn up to 92 percent of 4800 new words and phrases. Furthermore, he reports an average of 93.15 percent retention of foreign words and phrases learned after one year. Similar results and information regarding Lozanov's work was reported by Tashev and Natan (103).

Yotsukura (111) reports that in the Lozanov language course a student learns approximately 3000 new word groups. This corresponds with Bancroft's estimate of eighty to 100 words each day for twenty-five to thirty days of class. This is from two to three times faster than what is normally expected by traditional methods (Schuster, Bordon, and Gritton, 93).

Little information is available, as it relates directly to Lozanov's work regarding the potency of the individual components of the method when used in isolation or in various combinations. Here, it is necessary to turn to the small, but rapidly growing body of research available in the United States. At this time, much of the reliable research being reported is by the Iowa SALT organization under the direction of Dr. Donald Schuster at Iowa State University and other researchers.

In another study of Schuster's (88) several different types of suggestions and relaxation techniques were used as treatments while teaching Spanish words. These treatments were as follows:

1. *Conventional learning control:* Subjects were instructed to "learn any way you can."

2. *Sensory experience emphasis:* Subjects, under this condition,

were asked to experience the words as fully as possible. See them, hear them, taste them, feel them, or experience them as fully as possible.

3. *Preliminary physical exercise:* Subjects were given five minutes of Yoga-type exercises prior to the teaching lesson. Exercises such as bend-overs, side bending, back bending and wave of tension were used. (These exercises are described in Chapter 1.)

4. *Zen breathing:* Subjects were asked to attend to their breathing for five minutes prior to the Spanish lesson.

5. *Zen breathing plus learning suggestions:* Besides attending to breathing, it was suggested that the subjects would find the words pleasant and easy to learn and remember.

6. *Early pleasant learning recall (E.P.L.R.):* The student is instructed to return to a pleasant early learning experience that happened before learning was impaired. Subjects are asked to reexperience this fully.

Each experimental group was taught six lists of twelve different words that were carefully chosen so as to be of equal difficulty.

This study was a subjects-by-treatment analysis of variance design with six different subjects as replications. The six experimental conditions have already been explained.

The results of this study showed a main effect significant beyond the 1 percent level. While not statistically significant, E.P.L.R. produced retention of 37 percent better than the reference technique. (Learn any way.) The Sensory Experience technique was 14 percent better than the reference. (Learn any way.)

The results of this study indicated that the main effects were significant and that E.P.L.R. was worthy of further attention.

In another experiment at Iowa State University (Schuster, 89), effects of the alpha state (relaxed alert), indirect suggestion and word association techniques on learning rare English words were studied. Subjects were trained to produce the alpha state at will through use of biofeedback devices. E.P.L.R. was also used as the indirect suggestion treatment. Subjects were then asked to make unusual associations between rare words and its common synonym in an attempt to enhance memory function. The eight trained subjects were presented very carefully screened word lists to learn which were previously recorded on tape.

Students were asked to indicate if they already knew a rare word from the list of twelve so another could be substituted. Since this was within subjects, or subjects by treatment design, all subjects took all possible treatments.

The main effect of unusual word association was highly significant (P < .01). The interaction between suggestion (E.P.L.R.) and association was significant (P < .05) in that subjects did better when asked to make unusual association and recall a pleasant early learning experience. The alpha state condition did not provide significant results. However, it did provide for slightly improved learning when used in isolation rather than coupled to the other treatment variables.

Another study, using thirty-two male and female college-aged subjects was conducted by Bordon and Schuster (15) to investigate the influence of the following Lozanov components:

1. *Suggestion* — that learning was easy and would take place.

2. *Rhythmic breathing* — or breathing synchronized with presentation of material.

3. *Music* — with which breathing and rate of presentation were also synchronized.

This study was a between-subject full factorial analysis of variance design using the above-described treatment variables singly or in combination. There was also a no-treatment cell included in the study. Regardless of the treatment variable, all paired Spanish-English stimuli were present orally and visually at a rate of one pair every four seconds.

All sessions were followed by an immediate test of acquisition and a long-range test which occurred six weeks later. Data were analyzed by the number of correct responses using the analysis of variance technique. The results of the analysis indicated that the suggestion (easy learning) treatment showed a 60 percent improvement over the no-suggestion condition. The synchronized breathing condition showed a 47 percent improvement over the nonsynchronized breathing condition and the orchestrated music condition showed an improvement of 25 percent over the non-orchestrated presentation.

The best condition, however, was the combined treatments of synchronized breathing and orchestrated music which results in 78 percent better immediate acquisition than the nonsynchronized and nonorchestrated presentation condition.

As with immediate acquisition results, the main effects of the three treatment variables were significant (P < .01) in the case of long-range retention. The triple interaction term was also highly significant in long-range retention but not with the immediate acquisition. When no suggestion was given, synchronized breathing and orchestrated music interacted with favorable results, but the treatment seemed to fade in significance when combined with suggestion.

In pursuance of finding other applications for the Lozanov relaxation techniques, a study called Relaxation While Taking a Test was conducted at Iowa State University (Schuster, 90). The treatment used was Zen breathing and was the only relaxation technique employed. There were only four subjects available for this study, but each had been previously trained in the Zen relaxation approach.

The test content was material from the second quarter Spanish course with two forms (A & B) available. Each test was of equal difficulty level in the judgment of the experimenter. All subjects took both tests, one under the treatment condition and the other form under a no treatment condition. The tests were timed to exactly seventeen minutes. Subjects were assigned in a counterbalanced order presuming to assure that the effects of learning and fatigue would be distributed uniformly over all conditions. Analysis of variance was used to test the main effects.

While the results were not significant ($P < .05$), the results showed positive trends. The average test score was 62 percent under no treatment conditions and 68 percent under treatment conditions. It was suggested that further experimentation with more subjects would be warranted.

Peter Kline's work, as described in *The Washington Post* (March, 1974), is worthy of discussion. In a private school setting, the Sandy Springs School, Sandy Springs, Maryland, twenty-five high school students engaged in a program called Interlocking Curriculum. The objective of this program was to teach the traditional high school subjects in a way that their interrelatedness would be apparent to students (Kline, 53). The subjects that were integrated were English, mathematics, language, and fine arts.

The Sandy Springs projects, of which the 1973–1974 school year results are available, had the specific objective of applying some of the Lozanov techniques to create a thoroughly relaxed learning situation. The students were all individuals who had not been successful in the traditional high school setting. To recondition students who had been turned off to learning, Kline's experiment used the following techniques in an attempt to achieve their goals.

1. Silva mind control: This is based on Volpean relaxation approach whereby students are trained to produce their own states of physical and mental relaxation at will. This technique involves calling attention to each body part in sequence until the entire body is relaxed.

2. Music: Music was used extensively not only during learning sessions but as a matter of appreciation.

3. Nature method: Latin was taught by the nature method whereby words and phrases are taught without direct translation. That is, meanings of new words are grasped through context only.

4. Authority: The type of authority spoken of here is enlikened to the Lozanov definition. The teacher is to be a nonthreatening figure portraying prestige and inspiration.

5. Cooperative-caring atmosphere: The learning atmosphere was designed to be nonthreatening and love oriented. This was enhanced by what Kline (53) called a meaningful curriculum. Students were encouraged not to suppress feeling but rather to maintain complete openness with the staff.

The experimenters do not attempt to make scientific statements about the success of their curriculum as a whole or about the Latin language program. The results were evaluated against the background of former progress of the students involved.

When comparing the progress of twelve of the students during their second year at the Sandy Springs School, it was found that these students have made better than a year's progress. The average grade level had been 1.39 before entering the curriculum. By the beginning of the second year, the average overall grade equivalent had been raised to 2.64. Grades had improved considerably. This group had entered with predominantly failing grades but had risen to a larger percent of passing grades. There were fourteen "A's" and only four "F's" compared to the four "A's" and fourteen "F's" the students had earned in their earlier experiences.

All grade equivalent scores were obtained from the California Achievement Tests (Forms A & B, 1970 Edition).

It was found that many students had learned an equivalent of a year's Latin in five weeks with an average of three hours of study each day. Students were not taught English during the period they were receiving lessons in Latin. It was found that the basic understanding of the English language had also improved. This data was gathered by giving the California Achievement Test in English before and immediately following the Latin lessons.

The experimenter concluded his research report as follows (Kline, 53, p. 26):

> The observations in this monograph are by necessity speculative in nature and designed to provoke thought and experimentation rather than to state conclusions. It must be emphatically asserted that our experiment was inspired by the Lozanov method, but that it differed significantly from that method. No one who attempts similar experiments along the lines we have indicated, should claim that the Lozanov method is being used. The differences that are evident, from comparing the Jane Bancroft work, previously cited, with the observations cited above are sufficiently clear enough. The actual differences that emerge upon juxtaposition of the two methods will no doubt be even more substantial. Lozanov's work is the results of over twenty years of research and experimentation. Our method has been one of improvisation. We do not wish in any way to suggest that the methods are interchangeable, or that Lozanov's is not substantially superior in many important respects to the experiment we have described.

Bordon and Schuster (14) report another interesting study using only eight subjects between the ages of twenty to thirty-one years. Four of the students had some previous Spanish knowledge and four subjects did not. The subjects were trained in Yoga-type relaxation and were instructed to relax and listen to the music rather than the instructor during the ten three-and-one-half hour Spanish lessons. They had been told that suggestopaedia works but the words Yoga and suggestibility were not used directly. It was suggested however, that the subjects would learn the 900 words as easily as if they were young boys with all of their current abilities. A revolving crystal-like ball was provided for the students to look at during pretraining while thinking about their goals in the course.

Besides a fifteen-minute Yoga relaxation period and the presentation of materials while in the prone Savasana position, a fifty-minute oral practice period was provided each session.

Since this is a pretest/posttest/no-control-group design, the eight students were tested before and after the lessons. A one-hundred item test was provided by the Foreign Language Department at Iowa State University. The items were split in half by odd– and even-numbered items.

It was concluded from this study that the two major independent variables, previous knowledge of Spanish and the test condition interacted significantly at the .01 level of significance. Students who had no previous knowledge of Spanish surprisingly did better than those who had previous training. The researchers, through test-item analysis, were able to conclude the great differences between pre– and posttest scores were not due to a variance on difficulty levels of the tests or test-retest improvement. Thus, the difference was concluded to be due to the instructional process.

In the study described above, the subjects without some previous knowledge of Spanish went from 42 percent correct on the pretest to 82 percent correct on the posttest. Those having some previous Spanish went from 60 percent to 82 percent correct. These results spurred the researchers on to verify and elaborate on the results with a follow-up study (Bordon and Schuster, 14).

During this study suggestion was manipulated for (a) the relaxed learning of the content, (b) the relaxed recall of the content and (c) the conscious practice of the materials taught. The same design and procedures were used in this study as with the aforementioned. Ten male subjects, with a median age of 17.0, who had no previous knowledge of Spanish, participated in this study. The only reported modifications were as follows:

> (a) the delivery of suggestive messages during the dual stimulation pre-experimental training and during the preparation portion of the learning sessions, and (b) the manipulation of visual and voice-tonality suggestions during practice sessions, where the senior author used visual materials and voice tonality in a differential manner simultaneously.

Two forms of the test were given for both pre– and post– in a counterbalanced fashion. Half of the subjects took the odd form for the pretest and the even form for the posttest while the other half of the subjects did the opposite. There was no significance for the form of the test or the interaction of the testing. The only significant effect was the improvement in achievement scores from the pre– to the posttests (P < .05).

Again this study seems to point to some validity regarding the Lozanov approach and the positive effects of relaxation and learning suggestions.

Extensive study is now taking place in Bulgaria and other Soviet countries to add credence to the work of Dr. Lozanov. Biofeedback techniques are being used to measure brain activity during the memorization process. Work by Balevski (3) indicated that, while alpha brain wave activity does increase during memorization, an increase of more than 15 to 25 percent is not conducive to getting good results. He suggests use of intonation (previously discussed) and music to soothe brain bioelectric activity and thus increase the process of memorization. His study indicates that a relatively low level of brain activity appears to have a paradoxical effect of higher productivity. It appears however that suggestive instruction with intonation and music are less effective after reaching puberty (Balevski and Ganovski, 5). Upon entering puberty there seems to be a decrease in the effectiveness of suggestive instruction process particularly for short-range retention. According to these researchers sex does not seem to make a significant difference as to the effectiveness of the suggestive approach, although girls seem to do slightly better than boys on short-term memorization tasks. In any case students between the ages of eleven and seventeen do significantly better using suggestive techniques for memorization than the traditional rote method.

Smirnova (97) reports a study which took place at the State Pedagogical Institute in Moscow. The experimental group was taught by the Lozanov method, while the control group used a traditional method which was not described. The results of these French and English courses are given in terms of the volume of vocabulary learned in two months. The English experimental group had learned an average of 2550 words while the control group had learned an average 990 words. The French students had learned on the average of 2530 words during the experimental sessions while the control group achieved an average of 827 words. No levels of significance were given, nor information as to numbers of subjects or how they were assigned to groups. By the researcher's admission, other controls were absent. These weaknesses related to volume of materials and type of content presented to experimental and control groups since they were not identical. Also a great amount of out of class communication and sharing took place during the study. Control was, however, in evidence where the testing method was concerned. Students were tested both visually and orally using single words and short phrases.

It was also reported that the experimental group students made fewer mistakes per sentence than control groups. They also spoke faster. The experimental groups did worse than the control groups in spelling simply because they did less writing of new foreign words than control groups.

It was concluded by the staff involved in the experiment that the experimental groups were superior in their ability to converse and read aloud. The suggestopaedic approach had positive influence on the students in that learning was considered easier, much shyness was overcome, and creative activity was increased. The method, according to data presented, was also faster.

Another language study which reported the Lozanov method as being faster than the traditional methods was an experiment by Philipov (78) when comparing six students who were learning Bulgarian by the Lozanov method with ten students learning Russian the traditional way, there was such a marked difference that the study is worthy of mention. Little information is available about the study, but it again supports the Lozanov method as being an accelerated approach, since the experimental group learned about three times faster. It was also reported by experts who rated the students that the six Bulgarian students were significantly more proficient than the ten Russian students. The questionable aspect of this study appears to be the fact that two different languages were compared with each other.

A Canadian report (Racle, 81) seems to add further credence to the Lozanov methodology for the teaching of foreign language. Racle has instituted this approach for the teaching of French to English-speaking civil servants. While his work is not experimentally controlled, this author reports that students are learning the language much faster than ever before in the twenty-two half-day sessions. Using a test to evaluate a student's aptitude for learning a foreign language, he found the scores were raised considerably. The lowest scores had the largest gain (8.3 percent to 41.8 percent). Those who scored highest showed a smaller gain (59.7 percent to 86.9 percent). No significance levels were indicated.

Little information is available on the actual application of the Lozanov approach to the elementary school subjects. In a study in Sofia, Bulgaria, this approach was used for teaching reading in the primary grades (Lozanov, 63). Little information was available as to how the methodology was applied except that much of the suggestive procedure can be dispensed with since young children have not had their memories impaired. It appears that only part of this study is reportable since the experimental groups far excelled the control group in the pretest evaluation. This evaluation was subjective in nature since students were taped as they read. Data was recorded by denoting the percent of students who did not know letters, percent who knew letters, percent of students who could spell, percent of students who read in syllables or word by word, and students who read freely. It was not indicated who made these judgments. The portion of this study that was controlled to some degree involved subjects who could not read words at all but were at similar levels in their abilities to read letters. The experimental group consisted of twenty-six primary students and the control group consisted of twenty-five subjects at the onset of the study. They were recorded at the beginning of the year and again at the end of the school year. Ages of subjects were not given and exact procedure of how they were assigned to groups was not explained. When children were recorded reading from the text at the end of the study, it was judged that 25 percent of the experimental group read word by word while 55 percent of the control group read word by word. It was reported that 75 percent of the experimental group "read freely" while only 45 percent of the control group "read freely." A definition of "reading freely" was not provided except that it did not involve syllable-by-syllable or word-by-word reading and alluded to a fluent, free flowing type of performance. Overall, Lozanov reported favorable trends in the use of this methodology for the teaching of reading.

Prichard (79) reports a study applying the basics of the Lozanov method to remedial reading instruction. Twenty remedial students from ages seven to thirteen were randomly assigned from eligible subjects to a single treatment group. They were judged to be at least two years below their reading expectancy according to the Spache oral and silent reading scores. Pretest and posttest gain scores were compared to the subject's ability to master the basic relaxation techniques. The components of the Lozanov methods used were drama, music, rhythm, intonation, imagery, relaxation, and positive suggestion. These components were discussed earlier in this chapter.

It was concluded that large pretest-posttest gains were achieved for students who mastered the relaxation techniques and lesser gains for those who did not. The ability of the student to relax was judged by the researchers.

Overall, 80 percent of the participants gained a year or more on the Spache oral reading subtest while 75 percent of the subjects gained a year or more on the silent reading subtest after twelve weeks of instruction. Forty-five percent of the subjects gained a year or more on the Spache word recognition subtest.

When results are broken down in relation to the students' ability to relax it was found that those who attained an "excellent relaxation response" *all* gained a year or more on the Spache subtest. The only exception was one out of this group of eight who achieved less than a year on the word recognition subtest.

It was found that the remaining participants who achieved a "good relaxed" response also made favorable gains. Sixty-seven percent gained a year or more on the Spache oral and silent reading subtests while 50 percent made a year or more gain on the word recognition subtest.

Those participants who fell into the "poor relaxation response group" did not appear to do quite as well. Sixty-seven percent gained a year or more on the oral reading subtest, 50 percent gained a year or more on the silent reading subtest and only 17 percent showed this much gain on the word recognition test.

One weakness that appears to exist in this study is the subjectivity of determining the relaxation level. However, it was concluded that the overall gains previously described happened in twelve weeks of actual instruction and appeared to be most favorable. This study took place in the DeKalb County School District in the state of Georgia.

In a more recent study by Prichard and Taylor (79) favorable results were again reported using suggestopaedic components in a clinical setting in DeKalb County, Georgia. This author/researcher chose twenty students ages eight to thirteen who were two years behind in reading level. (Spache oral and silent reading subtest scores vs. Spache listening potential scores.) The experiment made use of previously described components of the Lozanov method such as relaxation techniques, positive suggestion, drama, music, intonation, rhythm, some synchronized breathing, active and passive phase sequencing. In summarizing their results it was found that the average gain made in fourteen weeks of instruction was two years on both the Spache oral and silent reading subtests. Word recognition gain scores were somewhat smaller as indicated by the Spache word recognition subtest. It should be mentioned that words from this subtest were not chosen to be taught. Rather Burnell Loft lists were used.

In a doctoral dissertation study reported by Held (37) the use of mild calming (Zen breathing) and Early Pleasant Learning Recall (E.P.L.R.) were examined when used singly and in combination. Sixty-four fifth and sixth grade students were the subjects. These subjects were divided into four groups and either received no treatment, E.P.L.R. treatment, Zen treatment, or the combination of E.P.L.R. and Zen. They were taught twelve rare English words and tested for immediate retention after each of the two sessions and one week later for delayed recall on the common meanings of these words. A factorial design was used as the statistical tool. A critical evaluation of that study follows.

Evaluation of the Study

Reading level appeared to be the most influential factor in this study since, in three out of the four criterion, reading level gained significance ($P < .01$). Spache and Spache (99), Bond and Tinker (13) and others support this finding. Better readers would be expected to learn new vocabulary with greater ease than poorer readers. Better readers generally have better word attack skills and a more highly developed visual memory and a richer background of experience.

Grade level reached significance only once and that was in delayed recall ($P < .05$). Since word difficulty was carefully controlled for all sessions it would appear that word difficulty level was not a confounding factor in that session. The fact that sixth graders were superior over fifth graders in only one word test is difficult to explain. Perhaps this happened by chance, or possibly it was due to the small number of subjects involved in the study. It is not too surprising, however, that the main effects of grade level were not highly significant throughout the study since the spread of reading abilities is so wide in those grades and not too dissimilar. Also, a study by Balevski and Ganovski (4) shows little difference between children of ages eleven and twelve in the effects of suggestion on short-term or long-term memory.

Sex differences did not reach significance in any of the dependent criterion. Again, this is not too surprising since Lozanov (64) originally claimed no sex differences in the effectiveness of this approach. More recent studies, however, do claim a slight edge for women in reproducing words learned (Balevski and Ganovski). There are few studies available on this topic at these two grade levels. Maccoby and Jacklin (65) in their research failed to find sex differences in elementary age children in suggestibility, ability to inhibit early incorrect learning, auditory and visual activities, or rote learning. A study by Balevski and Ganovski (4) shows slight differences in favor of girls for the effects of suggestion on short-term memory.

The main effects of treatment reached significance only once and that was in delayed recall (P < .05). Here E.P.L.R. and mind calming (Zen) were significant over the combination and no treatment. These transient results are difficult to understand since other researchers support their use (Schuster, 92; Bordon and Schuster and Gritton, 93).

Perhaps treatment exercises were not of proper duration and a longitudinal study is needed to test these treatment effects over time. Since this study was brief and had small numbers of subjects the results could have happened by chance. E.P.L.R. was, by itself, more consistently helpful since *all lower readers benefited* from it in both delayed recall tests. This would appear to be encouraging.

In spite of some beneficial results in the use of E.P.L.R. and mind calming, the combination of the two did not reach significance in the dependent variable in any session. Since the two treatments were beneficial in isolation one would expect compounding results. Again it is suggested that time was a contributing factor here. Longer treatment periods are probably needed. The time allowed for the combination was the same as for either treatment by itself, namely five minutes.

The only significant interactions in relation to treatments, grade, sex and reading level that emerged were a Reading by Grade by Treatment interaction (P < .05). Since this interaction appeared *twice*, and both in delayed recall, it appears to be worthy of further study. More research will be needed to try to determine why there was significant interaction in delayed recall and not in immediate recall.

The results of this study were both encouraging and discouraging because of their transient nature. Nevertheless, further research is warranted to answer questions this study provoked.

In another study relating directly to reading, Prichard (79) received encouraging results which support the use of suggesto-paedia for reading instruction. The study took place in a normal fifth grade class (N = 31) using procedures similar to what have been reported in this text, i.e., physical and mental relaxation techniques, music, drama, imagery, etc.

The study was conducted in a central Iowa school system with a specially trained teacher to do the instruction over a period of one year.

An analysis of covariance to evaluate the results was used with the dependent variable pretest as covariate to test the treatment vs. control effect. The dependent variables, reading comprehension, and vocabulary test scores showed significant results. The effect found for pretest and treatment was significant at the (P < .01) level with the result for gain in reading comprehension being the same. Significant effects were also found for both pretest (P < .01) and treatment on vocabulary scores (P < .05).

In the same report Prichard cited similar results in other studies that have taken place in Iowa that encourage the use of suggestopaedic-intuitive type approach.

Beer (8) in his excellent report, discussed the use of sug-gestopaedia in a Vienna public for two first grade classes (N = 64) in the teaching of reading, arithmetic, and writing over a period of 10 months (1973–74). He reports that there were no significant differences between the control group and experimental group in intelligence, vocabulary, picture test, or educational-professional background of the parents. The results were encouraging and reported as follows:

Arithmetic

The students achieved not only the first grade goals, but second and third grade materials were also taught successfully.

Reading

The purpose here was to bring the students to a high level of reading ability and comprehension. For this reason, they were given more reading materials than the other first grades. The results were highly encouraging since the goals were already reached by the end of the semester.

Writing

The results in this subject were encouraging as well, since all students achieved the first grade writing goals as well as part of the second grade goals.

It is important to mention here that Beer reported considerable satisfaction with the approach by parents, supervisors, and administrators. In other testing the psychologists found the children's calmness and balance "remarkable." Many other studies report these types of benefits as well.

An intensive effort to assist an identified learning disability child in reading improvement was reported by Held (38) in *The Journal of Suggestive-Accelerative Learning and Teaching*. This article is reprinted here to give the interested reader a complete picture of an incredible success story.

NOW JOHNNY CAN READ*
Introduction

A noticeable tension permeated the air the instant Johnny and his mother entered my office at Al Batin Academy in King Khalid Military City. They had just arrived in Saudi Arabia from Columbia, Maryland. Johnny's father had accepted a high position on a military project with the Saudi Arabian government.

Johnny avoided any direct glances. At first I thought he probably feared headmasters, but his mother exhibited evasive behavior as well. After exchanging niceties the whole truth came out. By then I had guessed it. Johnny had a serious problem, he could not read. Worse yet, he had been diagnosed as having a serious neurological dysfunction that interfered with his learning. Johnny could identify only a few initial consonants and it was obvious that both mother and son were extremely disturbed by the whole affair. It was difficult to determine which one was most upset, but later it was obvious that the mother took first place.

I did what I could to reassure them and get both of them to trust me. I offered to work with Johnny each day in my office. This offer of assistance was met with gratitude by the mother, but Johnny

*From Dean F. Held, Now Johnny Can Read, *The Journal of Suggestive-Accelerative Learning and Teaching, 4* (Fall):170–176, 1979. Courtesy of the editor.

reacted negatively. "Are you going to give me a test?" he asked. "No," I replied, "a test is unnecessary. We'll just have lots of fun and you'll see how easy it is to read." I offered Johnny's mother coffee and shared a Pepsi® with Johnny. We chatted about Saudi Arabia and soon both Johnny and his mother freely discussed their exciting trip.

Johnny and I liked each other immediately. I gave him every ounce of encouragement I could, as spontaneously as possible. I made my first appointment with Johnny, giving him a few days to adjust to his new environment.

It was quite obvious that formal diagnosis was out of the question. Johnny was seven years old and in first grade for the second time. His records indicated a high average IQ (WISC). His oral language development was not appreciably different from his peers. But he exhibited every type of avoidance technique I had ever encountered in my clinical work.

Since I generally view diagnosis as an "ongoing process," I gave no tests but made careful observations instead. I noticed that his visual and auditory discrimination appeared to be adequate, but he lacked skill in both visual and auditory memory. He was extremely "uptight," and had a very poor self-image and attitude about learning. This is a typical symptom and, as in other cases, I felt that the Lozanov techniques were exactly what this child needed. His former treatment had been very synthetic in nature and he could not "see the forest because of the trees."

Procedure

The parents

I conferred with Johnny's parents at length about Johnny's problems and their role in helping to resolve them. I asked them to refrain from discussing Johnny's problems in his presence and to give Johnny positive input at every opportunity, especially where self-image and learning were involved.

The classroom teacher

Johnny's classroom teacher became involved in the case. By careful consultation she reinforced everything I was attempting to do in the remediation sessions. She also made careful observations to facilitate the ongoing diagnosis.

The SALT sessions

I decided to try every technique I could find or develop to help Johnny overcome his fear of reading. The primary objective of each lesson was suggestive and de-suggestive in nature, designed to build a positive self-image and learning attitude. At the same time, the lessons were devised to de-suggest the barriers he had developed and to penetrate the protective shell with which he had surrounded himself. In time, I discovered this suggestopedic sequence which seemed to work best with Johnny.

1. *Preparation Phase* (5 minutes)

This was absolutely necessary in Johnny's case, so I used the various mind calming techniques available to us (i.e., white cloud, EPLR, deep breathing, etc.).

2. *Active Phase* (25 minutes)

I used language experience almost exclusively early in this session, followed by dramatic presentation of problem sounds and words with Johnny involved in repetition. These were words Johnny had difficulty remembering as he read his stories back to me. This will become clear as you study the lesson outlines.

3. *Passive Phase* (15 minutes)

During this final phase, I continually presented problems and easy words to Johnny with the triad of intonation. I used background music and rhythm with a special effort to keep time with it. Johnny's task was mainly to relax and listen to the music. (Note: As the following lesson samples indicate, I was very careful to integrate the content of all three phases into a meaningful whole. Thus, the activity in the preparation phase became the material for the active phase. Often the active phase was also psychodramatic in nature.)

The lessons

I began our endeavor by getting to know Johnny well; delving into his background of experiences, his deep feelings, his strengths and weaknesses, his likes and dislikes. Actually, this process started at the first encounter and continued throughout the remediation. A few sample lessons follow. (Note: I do not refer to my work as remedial or clinical to parents or students. Instead, I call whatever facility I am using an "Enrichment Workshop." The lessons are designed to be personally enriching and academically profitable.)

Lesson Plan: 1 Date:

New Name

Objectives:
    A. Reduce fear of making errors.
    B. Reduce avoidance techniques.
    C. Develop new self-image.
    D. Vehicle of suggestion/de-suggestion.
    E. Provide content for lesson.

Preparation Phase: (5 minutes)

    A. Deep breathing and positive suggestion.
    B. Discuss favorite heroes.
    C. Develop theme of who you would like to be.
Attributes are free of personal weaknesses and fears.

Active Phase: (25 minutes)

    A. Language experience student or teacher writes new biography (input from both).
    B. Student reads biography orally.
    C. Dramatic activity with problem words.
(Problem words are put on flash cards for use during the passive session.)
    D. Visual imagery practice.

Passive Phase: (15 minutes)

    A. Teacher uses dramatic approach to present words (music, intonation, rhythm).
    B. Student mentally visualizes words.
Note: Number of words learned is an outcome, not an objective.

Lesson Plan: 2 Date:

Continuation of New Name

Objectives:
    A. Mind calming.
    B. Reinforce new self-image.
    C. Bring about extinction of learning barriers.
    D. Develop memory.

Preparation Phase:

A. White cloud and positive suggestion.

B. Discuss new self (vehicle to facilitate new biography development in active phase).

Active Phase:

A. Language experience—finish new biography.
(Don't push this; use as many periods as necessary.)

B. Read biography, review words, learn new words from biography.

Passive Phase:

A. Teacher uses dramatic presentation of new words.

B. Student relaxes and develops mental images of words. (Music, intonation, and rhythm are used.)

Lesson Plan: 3 Date:

New Name Reinforcement

Objectives:

A. Reinforce affective aspects of new biography through suggestion.

B. Review total language part of biography (content).

Preparation Phase:

A. A mind calming activity. (This was, and continued to be, important for Johnny.)

Active Phase:

A. Teacher and student dramatize new words.

B. Allow rhythm to be a subtle syllabication process.

C. Read "whole" biography again.

Passive Phase:

A. Teacher-dramatic presentation of words (music, intonation and rhythm).

B. Student relaxes and visualizes words.

Lesson Plan: 4 Date:

Objectives:

A. Provide for mind calming and open mind.

B. Develop visual imagery (both fantasy and word visualization).

C. Provide for an intuitive learning vehicle.

Preparation Phase:

A. Do white cloud exercise.

B. Suggest fantasy trip to wherever the student wishes to go while in the cloud.

Active Phase:

A. Write about experience. (Teacher writes on chart paper and makes flash cards with key words from the story.)

B. Engage in visual imagery with words.

Passive Phase:

A. Teacher sings words to background music (rhythm, intonation).

B. Student attends to flash cards passively.

List of Suggested Imagery Activities

1. Have students imagine themselves being their favorite hero (experience the person wholly).

Objectives: Change self-image, raise learning expectations, create positive learning attitudes, and provide for language experience, incidental word attack, vocabulary development, other skills according to students' needs.

Suggestions:

You are as good as this favorite person of yours.

You can do anything you put your mind to.

He does everything easily, so can you. (The teacher must behave in such a way as to show students he or she really means it.)

2. Early Pleasant Learning Recall. (See earlier instructions.)

Objectives: Develop positive attitudes about learning, raise learning skills, and develop needed skills.

Suggestions:

Learning is easy and fun.

Relaxation engages your automatic learning devices and improves memory.

3. Hot air balloon trip. (See instructions detailed earlier.) Note: Taking imagery trips has countless possibilities as indicated by the objectives. The trips can also involve vehicles such as: white cloud, mountain top, flying saucer, magic carpet, hang glider, large bird, etc. The student can go anywhere he wishes and experience what he wishes with the teacher's help.

Objectives: Provide for deeper relaxation and vivid imagery, provide a vehicle for language experience, provide feelings of freedom from inhibition, provide for content of lesson, provide for concept development, and provide for remediation of word difficulties through follow-up activity.

Suggestions:

You will enjoy this trip and see many things.

You will learn many new words and how to spell them.

You will feel freer than ever before.

You can write whatever you feel.

You will learn and remember new words and reading skills.

4. New names and biography. Lozanov suggests this practice at the onset of corrective classes.

Objectives: Reduce fear of making errors, reduce avoidance techniques on the part of students, develop new self-concepts, develop positive learning attitudes, and raise learning expectations.

Suggestions:

Read about the new you.

He is everything you want to be and can be. (Note: The new biography is very carefully written by the teacher to fit the needs of the student in relation to his psychological setup.)

5. Word visualization. Take time for the student to mentally see problem words.

Objectives: Allow time for the student to integrate the spelling of a new word along with its meaning.

Suggestions:

See the whole word.

See the syllables.

See the whole word again.

You will remember the word. (Note: Do this with the Dolch words during an active and passive session.)

6. Read short but interesting stories to children. Have students vividly imagine characters, action, and endings. Have students reconstruct portions of the story. Stories should reflect interests and emotional needs. Children should always share feelings and ideas. Stories should be dramatic and exciting with both tragic and happy endings.

Objectives: Create interest and emotional need for reading, provide character identification, provide for emotional outlet, develop group unity and acceptance, develop appreciation for reading as an emotional experience, and provide a vehicle for vocabulary development.

Suggestions:
This story is exciting.
You will learn about life as it is (or is not).
You will enjoy doing something together, you're all equal, yet different.
You will see and appreciate the excitement of the story.
You will want to read stories like this.

7. Vividly imagine an emotional experience. It might be happy, sad, exciting, or nerve-wracking. Write about the experience and share it with peers. (Note: This should be a series of lessons — writing happy, then sad, stories followed by other stories of varied emotional tones.)

Objectives: Provide the student an opportunity to express his emotions and share with others, provide new insights into self, provide for group belonging, provide a stimulus for language experience, provide a vehicle for vocabulary development, and reduce hostility toward those who have hurt him.

Suggestions:
We've all had good and bad experiences.
We are all more alike than different.
By sharing we can help each other.
We can learn from each other.

8. Situational activity whereby the group solves specific problems as a team. Example: You are all members of a fire department. A young boy crawled to the top of a large tree. Together you must plan a way to get him down. First write your individual plan, then get together and come up with a written master plan. (Note: These activities should be reported using Police Department problems, medical teams, etc.)

Objectives: Provide for group interaction, acceptance and cooperation, provide a stimulus for language experience, provide content for remedial instruction, provide stimulus for reading, reduce avoidance and withdrawal tendencies, and develop ease in writing ideas down.

Suggestions:

By putting your ideas together you can solve problems.

You can learn new ideas and words from each other.

Everyone's ideas are worthy.

Any idea can easily be written down.

This list outlines other activities I used. The teacher must always adapt the activity to fit both the psychological and academic needs of the child. In Johnny's case, the academic outcomes were very automatic. He learned to read to expectancy level in a very short time. There were some important factors I had to keep in mind in Johnny's case, and my approach had to reflect these.

A. Johnny was extremely "uptight" and exhibited failure syndromes and avoidance techniques. Therefore, mind calming activities were essential and helpful.

B. Professional neurological reports indicated mental process dysfunction. This is not necessarily a problem if the child is allowed to compensate. However, his former treatment involved only crash phonics programs which often inhibit the compensatory process. Thus, the whole word approach was used and any phonics that were taught were incidental, if not accidental.

C. Careful integration of the content from the preparation phase to the passive phase was essential. Johnny has to see the "whole" and process its parts in his own way.

D. Transition to the textbook has to be successful. I had promised him he would learn to read easily. This moment of moving into books was crucial. I chose a primer level Scott-Foresman and exposed Johnny to the vocabulary in conjunction with his language experience without his knowledge of it. He flew through his first book in a few minutes. From then on his learning barriers reached extinction as he read, read, and read. I continued to expose him to difficult vocabulary prior to actual book assignment. Thus, vocabulary control on the part of the teacher is essential.

E. Intensive practice with visual imagery proved to be important in Johnny's case.

F. Carefully placed positive suggestion continued to be important. The more subtly presented, the more effective it proved to be.

G. Lessons had to be carefully planned and standard rituals were in order. Johnny needed to structure his learning environment.

H. The use of music, rhythm, and intonation were in order for each lesson to facilitate easy memory.

Summary

Johnny arrived at Al Batin Academy in early March of 1978 without any functional reading skills. Some facilitative factors did exist, i.e., desire to read, auditory and visual discrimination, intelligence, etc.

Unfortunately, Johnny left the academy in early June. But in three months Johnny had gone from a nonreader to a fluent reader at a second grade level. No follow-up has been possible, but at Christmas time of 1978, I received a letter from his mother saying that Johnny was doing much better.

Johnny's self-image, attitude toward learning, and reading skills have improved appreciably. Whether he was able to hang on to his "new self" remains to be seen.

Nelson (70) in his thorough report on the application of Lozanov's approach to learning disability had encouraging commentary about its use in that field. The article is a fine overview of the suggestopaedic approach and its application in that field which closely approximates this author's work.

Nelson's study applied and tested the effectiveness of the suggestopaedic approach with six-, seven-, and eight-year-old subjects who had learning problems. The research question was as follows: "For six– to eight-year-old learning disabled children, is there a difference between the effectiveness of the Lozanov approach versus the traditional approach in facilitating retention of unknown words?"

The sample was small (N = 5), but again significant results were found (P < .05) as it relates to the above question and encourages continued research and application.

Summary*

The body of research supporting the application of suggesto-paedia to reading and learning disability appears to be strong enough, even though certainly not complete, to encourage its continued use. Whether it is called suggestopaedia, the intuitive approach or SALT matters little. One must remember, too, that this is a "human approach" and not all successes should be measured in levels of significance from computer programs. The experience of caring practitioners, their subjective evaluations and highly motivated involvement have great value too. Caskey (21) put it superbly when he stated, "Let's hope advocates will keep calm long enough to conduct meaningful research. Without research, of course, suggestology will continue to be lumped with far-out sounding consciousness altering techniques known more for their rigamarole than their substance."

---

*Readers interested in additional research studies and more information regarding this methodology, can gather a host of information by contacting the Society for Suggestive-Accelerative Learning and Teaching (SALT), Psychology Department, Iowa State University, Ames, Iowa, 50011, Dr. Donald Schulter.

APPENDIX

The following puppetry ideas have actually been tried with students and represent a collection of puppetry activity cards created by Robert Jansen (45) and his teacher education students. They are included here, with his permission, because of the in-depth description of use, objective, and construction.

Sock Puppet

Grade: Kindergarten   *Source Person:* Gail Caudle
Curriculum Area: Emotions
Time: 20 minutes
Goals: To learn about emotions and expressions, to have fun, to learn to use puppets to make expressions.
Materials: Sock, buttons, needle and thread, glue, fabric and scraps, trims, construction paper, felt scraps.
General Objectives: Given a sock and materials the student will construct a puppet using the sock; the student will be able to make the puppet show emotion through expression and movement.
Construction Procedures: Take a sock, pull on hand, tuck the end of the sock back into the palm of your hand. Decide where features will go and mark, remove from hand, attach buttons, fabric, etc. For features, with glue or thread, pull on hand, tuck mouth (attach if you wish).
Curriculum Inclusion Procedures: Put out Raggedy Ann book about *Happy Sad.* Read to children, talk about being happy and sad, how can you tell if someone is happy or sad, angry, hurt, tired, etc. Have children show happy and sad face, demonstrate and suggest other emotions; bring out pictures and drawing of *Happy Sad*, mad, hurt faces for children to identify. Talk about using a puppet to show

emotions, helping other children show emotion.

Activity: Construct puppets. Have children use puppets to make expressions about how they feel, how they think, how others feel. Make puppet angry, sad, happy, hurt. Have children use puppet to show an emotion and have the rest of the class guess what it is.

Shadow Puppet

Grade: Special Ed—
   Learning Disabilities   Source Person: Sherilyn Ritchie
Curriculum Area: Creative Writing
Time: 30 minutes
Goals: To dramatize and encourage their writing.
Materials: Cardboard from stockings or sheets or shirts, scissors, pencil, gel, plastic straw, 24–26 gauge wire, glue, masking tape.
General Objective: Each child will write a story and make a puppet, using his puppet to act out the story.
Construction: (1) Draw the character on the card and cut out. (2) Outline and/or fill in cutouts with gel and glue onto back of card. (3) Poke wire through straw one-half inch from the end, bend wire to lie next to straw. (4) Poke wire through card and bend in opposite (up-down) direction, tape ends down.
Curriculum: (1) Have a shadow show presented to the class. (2) Discuss shadow puppets, their construction, and use. (3) Make puppets. (4) In groups of two or three, have the children write stories. (5) Perform the stories using the puppets.

Pop-up Puppet

Grade: 3   *Source Person:* Robert Jansen
Curriculum Area: Art, language arts
Time: 2 hours
Goals: Because there is no restriction on the choice of puppet characterization, the construction of this puppet will hopefully lead to an increased awareness of personal interests. A freedom of artistic expression should be realized in the use of the puppet.

Materials: Cone; Styrofoam® ball (head), diameter should be smaller than cone opening; stick (1½ to 2 feet long and approximately one-half inch wide). Miscellaneous materials: Paint, material, construction paper, yarn, paste, scissors.

General Objectives: At the end of the session child will have completed a pop-up puppet made to his or her own specifications and desires. Children will use their puppets in groups of 2–4 at a time in improvisational situations at the leader's suggestion.

Construction Procedures: (1) Choose a characterization for puppet — any person, animal, "animate" inanimate object, etc. (2) Gouge out hole in Styrofoam for stick. (3) Cover "head" with material, sew on "button" features, paste on yarn mouth and hair, add other embellishments. (4) Apply glue in hole and attach stick. (5) Glue, sew, or tape garment onto stick from neck. (6) Paint or cover cone with foil or construction paper. (7) Insert puppet into cone. (8) Add a thickness of tape to the bottom of stick (optional) to keep puppet securely anchored in cone.

Curriculum Inclusion Procedure: The object of this puppet construction and improvisation is (1) fun, and (2) the catharsis which accompanies psychodrama. The child is able to express ideas through the puppet he might ordinarily repress, especially as this particular puppet has a built-in safety valve (disappearing act).

Stick Puppet

Grade: Kindergarten—primary   *Source Person:* Susan Baird
Curriculum Area: Social studies
Time: 30–45 minutes (2 sessions)
Goals: To acquaint children with a creative dramatics experience using puppets.
Materials: Stick, construction paper, crayons, scissors.
General Objectives: The child will be able to utilize a stick puppet.
Construction Procedures: Puppet head is constructed using construction paper, scissors, and crayons. Now glue to top of stick.
Curriculum Inclusion Procedures: Pre-activity—read the story *The Three Little Pigs.* Discuss story.
Activity: Construct puppet.

Follow-up: Re-read story, discuss with children the characters and story plot. Setup a stage; choose children to portray characters; children retell story using puppets.

Coat Hanger (Rod) Puppet

Grade: 1   *Source Person:* Gail Caudle

Curriculum Area: Language arts

Time: 30 minutes

Goals: To teach and reinforce the "F" sound, to improve self-image, and to use complete sentences.

Materials: Coat hangers, nylons, buttons, wire, needle and thread, felt scraps, glue, pipe cleaners, yarn.

General Objectives: (1) Having constructed a stick puppet of a cat, the child will make the angry cat sound and use a word which begins with the correct sound. (2) Given the cat puppet the student will play the game of Minister's Cat using the proper letter of the alphabet in a complete sentence.

Construction Procedures: (1) Bend the coat hanger into the desired shape. (2) Pull nylon over the hanger and tie the bottom. (3) Pick out materials for eyes, nose, mouth, hair, and ears. (4) Glue, sew or wire in place.

Curriculum Inclusion Procedures: (1) Display books and pictures about cats. Read one of the books. (2) Discuss characteristics of cats and words which describe cats using each letter of the alphabet. (3) Play the Minister's Cat. (4) Read another book about cats. Discuss which was the funniest, fattest, most colorful, etc., and how they might sound and act. (5) Bring out materials and discuss how they might be used. (6) Construct the puppets. May work in groups. (7) Review the characteristics of cats and play the Minister's Cat using the puppets. (8) Talk about the angry cat sound and introduce the "F" sound. (9) Have each child use his puppet and make the angry cat sound. (10) Have children use words in complete sentences. Later have children use as many words which begin with "F" as possible in a complete sentence.

Stick Puppet

Grade: Kindergarten and 6th   *Source Person:* Andra Tremper
Curriculum Area: Community helpers, food types
Time: 2 hours
Goals: 6th grade: Self-confidence, sense of achievement, positive
    feelings about helping others. Kindergarten: Make them
    more aware of their eating habits, drama appreciation.
Materials: Paper towel tubes, 2 paper plates, glue, scissors, paint
    stirrers (sticks), felt scraps for features, tissue paper in
    different colors, yarn scraps.
General Objectives: 6th grade: Learn how to put on a puppet show.
    Kindergarten: Learn about vegetables and how they help
    our body.
Construction Procedures: Tomato: (1) Staple two paper plates front
    to front, insert stick in one end, staple on. (2) Cut out red
    tissue the size of plate, glue on. (3) Cut out felt features,
    tissue stem, glue. Carrot: (1) Cut orange tissue in carrot
    shape, wrap around paper towel tube, glue. (2) Extend part
    of tissue below tube. (3) Cut slit in back for stick. (4) Insert
    stick, glue, cut felt tissue features, glue. (5) Fringe one end
    of a tissue rectangle. (6) Roll up and glue inside top of
    paper tube.
Curriculum Inclusion Procedures: The sixth graders will construct
    the puppets, write a script and present it to the kindergarten.
    This activity will reinforce what *they* have learned about
    community helpers. They now have an opportunity to be
    "helpers" themselves. It is also a way to teach puppetry
    construction skills, creative writing, and dramatic skills.

    The students will be able to watch a puppet show teach-
    ing them about vegetables and how they help your body to
    grow. This is one creative way they can learn about differ-
    ent kinds of food. It is a nice change from listening to the
    teacher talk. The kids become involved!

Sock Puppet

Grade: Kindergarten   *Source Person:* Susan Baird
Curriculum Area: Social studies
Time: 30–45 minute session (2 sessions)

Goals: To acquaint children with a creative dramatics experience using puppets.

Materials: Sock, glue, buttons, yarn, red felt.

General Objectives: The child will be able to utilize a sock puppet.

Construction Procedures: (1) With sock push toe in three inches, cut 3″ × 6″ rectangle of red felt, glue to "pushed in toe" and let dry. (2) Glue eyes (buttons or bottle caps), let dry. (3) Add yarn for hair.

Curriculum Inclusion Procedure: Activity: Construct puppets.

Follow-up: Everyone uses puppets to sing familiar songs (vocabulary development).

Stick Puppet

Grade: 1–4   *Source Person:* Janet Billington

Curriculum Area: Affective and creative writing

Goals: The students will develop an awareness of self and develop a positive self-image.

General Objectives: After a student has constructed a puppet and has been involved in a discussion on individuality, he will think of himself as more of a person.

Construction Procedures: (1) Bend wire to desired shape. (2) Stretch nylon over it. (3) Stuff with nylons, cotton or newspaper. (4) Cut out shapes of head from fabric, sew or glue on. (5) Sew on buttons for eyes. (6) Make hair from yarn; sew or glue on. (7) Draw on nose, mouth, and cheeks.

Curriculum Inclusion Procedures: To show that no two puppets or children are alike. Have students make the puppets. When finished have them hold them up and look at all of them. Discuss the fact that they are all different, no two of them are alike. Have the students write their name and look at it. Talk with them about the fact that they are not like anyone else in the world and how glad they should be to be themselves. The following is a little poem that fills in nicely:

> Nobody sees what I can see,/ For back of my eyes there is only me. And nobody knows how my thoughts begin,/ For there is only me inside my skin. Isn't it strange how everyone owns,/ Just enough skin to cover his bones? My father's would be too

big to fit,/ I'd be all wrinkled inside of it. And my baby brother's is much too small,/ It just wouldn't cover me at all. But I feel just right in the skin I wear,/ And there is nobody like me anywhere.

If you want to expand this to a creative writing lesson, you could have them write a story about "How it Feels to be Me."

Sock Puppet

Grade: 3   *Source Person:* Janet Billington
Curriculum Area: Science
Time: 45 minutes
Goals: For the student to have the experience of expressing himself through construction of a puppet and use the puppet to reinforce concepts he has learned about sea life.
Materials: Sock, yarn or rope, buttons, needle, and thread.
General Objectives: Given instruction on a variety of sea life and constructing their sea creature they will list three reasons why sea life is important to man.
Construction Procedures: (1) Sew buttons on sock for eyes and nose. (2) Sew cord on a rope around for the mouth. (3) Sew a ribbon on or decorate any way you choose, trying to gain characteristics of sea creature.
Curriculum Inclusion Procedures: After a discussion of sea life and its importance to man have the students construct their own puppet. They can use the puppets in small groups or in front of the whole class telling what sea creature they have made, what it eats, and how it is important to man.

Soup Box Puppet

Grade: 3   *Source Person:* Janet Billington
Curriculum Area: Science—social studies
Time: 30 minutes
Goals: For the students to have the experience of constructing a puppet; and to demonstrate a point about weather (seasons).
Materials: Cup of soup box, 2 pipe cleaners, rubber bands, masking tape, glue, cotton balls, black felt, eyelashes.

General Objectives: After a discussion on winter and winter weather and the construction of a snowman puppet the students will be able to list five changes that take place in nature from summer to winter as indicated by the teacher.

Construction Procedures: (1) Reinforce box top and bottom with masking tape. (2) Determine center of box and punch hole with ball-point pen. (3) Break pipe cleaner in half. Put one piece through end of rubber band and twist, the other end is connected to the other end and twisted. (4) From inside of box punch or push down ends of pipe cleaner through, spread out and tape down. Same at other end. Cover box with cotton balls. Cut eyes, nose, buttons from felt and glue on.

Curriculum Inclusion Procedures: During unit on weather when you are studying seasons make the snowman puppet. The students will have their puppets tell under what conditions they may be found, describe what snow is and what will eventually happen to the snowman.

Shadow Puppet

Grade: 1   *Source Person:* Maureen Sears
Curriculum Area: Spelling
Goals: Beginning writing skills.
Materials: Colored construction paper, plastic straws, 24–28 inch gauge wire, scissors.
General Objective: After having made the shadow puppet each child will be able to use it to identify a letter of the alphabet.
Construction Procedures: (1) Cut construction paper into desired letter. (2) Make two small holes in straw opposite each other. (3) Put wire through straw make two small holes in your letter. (4) Put wire through construction paper. (5) Fold back and tape ends of wire.
Curriculum Inclusion Procedures: (1) Talk about letters in the alphabet. (2) Learn alphabet song. (3) Build puppets. (4) Put on small puppet show with puppets singing alphabet song. (5) Use for singing classes (do-re-mi-fa).

String Puppet

Grade: 3   *Source Person:* Maureen Sears

Curriculum Area: Nature—science

Goals: Awareness of animals and life around them.

Materials: Construction paper (colored), scissors, Elmer's® glue, envelopes, newspapers, string. Optional: Cotton balls, fabric scraps.

General Objectives: Having built the string puppet each child will be able to use his puppet to help him demonstrate his knowledge of its place in nature.

Construction Procedures: (1) Cut main body out of manila envelope. (2) Cut head about half the size of the body. (3) Cut two small circles half the size of the head for feet. (4) Cut small circle for tail. (5) Cut two long strips about as long as body for ears. (6) Repeat the above tracing twice onto desired color construction paper. (7) Glue matching sizes of construction paper on either side of an already cut manila envelope. (8) Glue feet, tail, ears, head in proper places. (9) Tightly roll newspaper and tape closed to make a rod. (10) Repeat number nine. (11) Tie on string onto one rod. (12) Connect loose end of string to tail. (13) Tie two strings of equal length to second role. (14) Connect to ears. (15) Optional: Glue cotton balls to either side of construction paper to make fluffy rabbit.

Curriculum Inclusion Procedures: (1) Talk about animals and how they get around. Example: How does a rabbit move? (It hops.) (2) Take a nature walk. (3) Talk again about what you saw on the walk. (4) Build string puppets. (5) Demonstrate how puppets get around. (6) Put on small puppet show (the Farmer in the Dell?). (7) Have a parade of animals. (8) Write about a favorite animal.

Sock Puppet

Grade: Special Ed—Learning
    Disabilities (middle ages)   *Source Person:* Sherilyn Ritchie

Curriculum Area: Puppetry

Time: 20 minutes

Goals: Introduction to puppetry and develop oral language.

Materials: Sock, one color; two of another color of buttons; needle, thread, scissors.

General Objectives: Each child will make a sock puppet and use it to talk to the class and/or other puppets.

Construction Procedures: (1) Sew one button in base of mouth. (2) Sew matching button on top for eyes.

Curriculum Inclusion Procedures: (1) Discuss sock puppets, various decors and uses. (2) Make puppets. (3) Discuss ways to use puppets. (4) Allow each child to have his puppet speak to the class, alone or with other puppets.

Coat Hanger Puppet

Grade: Kindergarten   *Source Person:* Susan Baird

Curriculum Area: Oral language development

Time: Thirty-minute lessons for five days

Goals: To promote self-esteem through the use of language and a common experience base.

Materials: Per child: One nylon panty hose, one coat hanger, an assortment of materials such as string, yarn, bottle caps, buttons, material scraps, felt, large seeds, white glue, and scissors.

General Objective: The child will gain practice in using his natural language while working with puppets.

Construction Procedures: (1) Bend coat hanger to desired shape. (2) Stretch nylon panty hose over coat hanger. (3) Let children choose from a selection of various materials to make faces using white glue and scissors to create what they want.

Curriculum Inclusion Procedure: (Three thirty-minute lessons) Pre-activities: After two days of many activities concerning self-concept, some of which could be: (1) Self-portraits, (2) experience charts, (3) reading stories related to self-image, (4) singing songs, (5) getting acquainted games and more. Thirty-minute activity: Motivation; read story "Faces" look into a mirror and talk about color, shape, parts of face, media child will be working with in creating puppets; construct puppet. Thirty-minute follow-up: Provide time for children to use puppets to talk to each other.

Pop-up Puppet

Grade: 1 or older   *Source Person:* Maureen Sears
Curriculum Area: Language arts
Time: 2 hours construction
Goals: Stimulus for writing and speaking.
Materials: Cone (approximately 18 inches), stick to fit through
    cone, newspaper, small Styrofoam ball, small colored but-
    tons, pipe cleaners, feathers, glue, color crayons.
General Objectives: Having built the pop-up puppet, each child
    will use his puppet as a story stimulus for monster stories.
Construction Procedures: (1) Color cones. (2) Put stick through
    cone. (3) Glue Styrofoam ball on top end of stick. (4) Tear
    newspaper into thin strips. (5) Glue onto Styrofoam ball at
    top and leave strips of paper hanging. (6) Tape bottom of
    stick so it won't slide through cone. Optional: Button eye
    or eyes, feathers, pipe cleaner antlers.
Curriculum Inclusion Procedures: (1) Read a story about a bad
    monster. (2) Read a story about a good monster. (Not all
    monsters are bad.) (3) Discuss monsters from stories.
    (4) Build puppets. (5) Discuss puppets from the class (are
    they mostly good or mostly bad monsters). (6) Use in class;
    when they want to ask questions have them hold up their
    cone and pop-up their monster. (7) While singing rounds
    keep puppet down until it's your turn to join in, then
    pop-up ("Row, Row, Row Your Boat"). (8) Have kids pair
    up and make up (in their heads) what their monsters did.
    (9) Have each pair stand up and tell their story, one pup-
    pet talks at a time while the other is down.

Finger Puppet

Grade: Special Ed—Learning
   Disabilities (young ages)   *Source Person:* Sherilyn Ritchie
Curriculum Area: Music-finger plays
Time: 10 minutes
Goals: To help visual finger play and to help guide creative
    musical expression.
Materials: Construction paper, masking tape, felt pen.

General Objectives: Each child will make a finger puppet and use it to demonstrate a finger play.

Construction Procedures: (1) Have child cut construction paper the width of child's thumb length and as long as two times around the child's thumb. (2) Have child tape paper rolled to size of child's thumb. (They may have to help one another.) (3) Have child draw eyes, nose, mouth, etc., on paper roll.

Curriculum Inclusion Procedures: (1) Make puppets. (2) Use puppets in learning song. (3) Sing song: "Where Is Thumbkin?" "Where is Thumbkin? Where is Thumbkin? Here I am! Here I am! How are you today, sir? Very well, I thank you. Run and hide. Run and hide."

BIBLIOGRAPHY

1. Alexander, J. Estill and Filler, Ronald Claude. *Attitudes and Reading*. Newark: International Reading Association, 1976.
2. Astor, Martin H. "Transpersonal Counseling as a Form of Transcendental Education." *Counseling and Values 29* (February 1975): 75–81.
3. Balevski, P. "EEG Changes in the Process of Memorization Under Ordinary and Suggestive Conditions." *Suggestology and Suggestopaedia 1* (January 1975).
4. Balevski, P., and Ganovski, L. "The Volume of Short-Term Memory at the Beginning of the Course and the Proficiency of Students Learning Foreign Languages by the Suggestopaedic System." *Suggestology and Suggestopaedia 2* (February 1975): 22–28.
5. Balevski, P., and Ganovski, L. "The Effect of Some of the Means of Suggestion on the Short-Term and Long Term Memory of Students from 11 to 17 Years." *Suggestology and Suggestopaedia 1* (March 1975): 47–52.
6. Bancroft, Jane W. "Foreign Language Teaching." *Canadian Modern Language Review 28* (1972): 9–13.
7. Bancroft, Jane W. "The Lozanov Language Class," *The Journal of Suggestive-Accelerative Learning and Teaching 1* (Spring 1976): 48–74.
8. Beer, Franz. "Report on the School Experiment-Suggestopaedia in Elementary School." *The Journal of Suggestive-Accelerative Learning and Teaching 3* (Spring 1978): 21–37.
9. Berry, Althea. "Implementing Major Instructional Factors." *Reading and the Elementary School Curriculum*. Edited by David L. Shepard. Newark, Delaware: I.R.A., 1969.
10. Biehler, Robert F. *Psychology Applied to Teaching*. Boston: Houghton-Mifflin Company, 1974.
11. Blitz, Barbara. *The Open Classroom*. Boston: Allyn and Bacon, Inc., 1973.
12. Blume, Robert. "Humanizing Teacher Education." *Phi Delta Kappan 52* (March 1971): 413.
13. Bond, Guy, and Tinker, Miles. *Reading Difficulties: Their Diagnosis and Correction*. New York: Appleton-Century-Crofts, Meredith Corporation, 1967.
14. Bordon, R. Benitez, and Schuster, Donald H. "Foreign Language Learning Via the Lozanov Method: Pilot Studies." *The Journal of Suggestive-Accelerative Learning 1* (Spring 1976): 3–15.
15. Bordon, R. Benitez, and Schuster, Donald H. "The Effects of a Suggestive Learning Climate, Synchronized Breathing and Music, on the Learning

and Retention of Spanish Words." *The Journal of Suggestive-Accelerative Learning and Teaching 1* (Spring 1976): 27–40.

16. Borg, Walter R., and Gall, Meridith D. *Educational Research: An Introduction.* New York: David McKay, Inc., 1971.

17. Bruner, Jerome. *The Process of Education.* New York: Vintage Books, 1960.

18. Buchanan, Marcia M. "Preparing Teachers to be Persons." *Phi Delta Kappan 52* (June 1971): 614–617.

19. Burron, Arnold, and Claybaugh, Amos L. *Basic Concepts in Reading Instruction: A Programmed Approach.* Columbus, Ohio: Charles E. Merrill Publishing Company, 1972.

20. Carroll, John B.; Davies, Peter; and Richman, Barry. *Word Frequency Book.* New York: Houghton-Mifflin Company, 1971.

21. Caskey, Owen L., "Suggestology in the United States." *The Journal of Suggestive-Accelerative Learning and Teaching 1* (Fall 1977): 105–117.

22. Chaney, D. S., and Andreasen, L. "Relaxation and NeuroMuscular Control and Changes in Mental Performance Under Induced Tension." *Perceptual Motor Skills 34* (April 1972): 677–678.

23. Charles, C. M. *Teacher's Petit Piaget.* Belmont, Calif.: Fearon Publishers, 1974.

24. Church, Joseph. *Language and the Discovery of Reality.* New York: Random House, 1961.

25. Coleman, Donavon E. *School Failure: A Tragedy You Can Help Your Child Avoid.* New York: Vantage Press, 1971.

26. Combs, Arthur W. *The Professional Education of Teachers.* Boston: Allyn and Bacon, Inc., 1965.

27. Combs, Arthur W.; Avila, D. L.; and Purkey, W. W. *Helping Relationships.* Boston: Allyn and Bacon, Inc., 1971.

28. Combs, Arthur W. *Educational Accountability: Beyond Behavioral Objectives.* Washington, D.C.: Association for Supervision and Curriculum Development, 1972.

29. DeBruin, Hendrik C. "Personality Concepts in Relation to Quality Teaching." *Teacher 89* (March 1969): 241–243.

30. Dilley, Josiah S. "Mental Imagery." *Counseling and Values 19* (February 1975): 110–115.

31. Ekwall, Eldon E. and Shanker, James L., *Diagnosis and Remediation of the Disabled Reader.* Boston: Allyn & Bacon, Inc., 1983.

32. Fattu, N. *N.E.A. Report of the National Commission on Teacher Education and Professional Standards.* Washington, D.C.: New Horizons in Education, 1964.

33. Flanders, N. A. "Personal-Social Anxiety as a Factor In Experimental Learning." *Educational Research Journal 45* (October 1951): 100–110.

34. Fromm, Erich. "Value Psychology and Human Existence." *New Knowledge in Human Values.* Edited by A. H. Maslow. Chicago: Henry Regnery Co., 1959.

35. Frost, Joe L., and Rowland, Thomas G. *Curricula for the Seventies.* Boston: Houghton-Mifflin Company, 1969.

36. Gould, Julius, and Kolb, William L. *A Dictionary of the Social Sciences.* New York: The Free Press, 1967.

37. Held, Dean F. "The Effects of the Lozanov Method for Teaching Word Meaning to Fifth and Sixth Graders." Unpublished dissertation, Iowa State University, 1975.

38. Held, Dean F. "Now Johnny Can Read." *The Journal of Suggestive-Accelerative Learning and Teaching 4* (Fall 1979): 170–176.

39. Hewitt, James. *Yoga and You*. New York: Pyramid Books, 1968.

40. Holt, John. *How Children Fail*. New York: Pitman Publishing Co., 1967.

41. Hudnut, Joseph. *Architecture and Spirit of Man*. Cambridge: Harvard University Press, 1949.

42. Hughes, Langston. *The First Books of Rhythms*. New York: Franklin Watts, Inc., 1954.

43. International Reading Association. *Intersensory Transfer, Perceptual Shifting, Modal Preference, and Reading*. Newark, New Jersey: International Reading Association, 1972.

44. Jackson, Philip W. *Life in Classrooms*. New York: Holt, Rinehart & Winston, 1968.

45. Jansen, Robert. "Collection of Puppetry Ideas." Unpublished collection, Scholastica College, 1978.

46. Johnson, Doris J., and Myklebust, Helmer R. *Learning Disabilities: Educational Principles and Practices*. New York: Grune & Stratton, 1964.

47. Joyce, Bruce R. *New Strategies for Social Education*. Chicago: Science Research Associates, Inc., 1972.

48. Karlin, Robert. *Teaching Reading in the High School*. New York: The Bobbs-Merrill Company, Inc., 1972.

49. Katz, Lillian G. "Perspectives on Early Childhood Education." *The Educational Digest* 39 (October 1973): 15–17.

50. Kelley, Earl C. "Another Look at Individualism." *The Helping Relationship Sourcebook*. Boston: Allyn & Bacon, Inc., 1971.

51. Kirk, R. *Experimental Design: Procedures for the Behavioral Sciences*. Belmont: Brooks Cole Publishing Co., 1969.

52. Klausmeier, Herbert J., and Goodwin, William. *Learning and Human Abilities*. New York: Harper & Row Publishers, 1966.

53. Kline, Peter. "The Sandy Spring Experiment: Apply Relaxation Techniques to Education." *The Journal of Suggestive-Accelerated Learning and Teaching 1* (Spring 1976): 16–26.

54. Kneller, George F. *Introduction to the Philosophy of Education*. New York: John Wiley and Sons, Inc., 1964.

55. Koff, Robert H. *Teacher Education is a Four Letter Word*. Chicago: American Educational Research Association, 1972.

56. Lee, Dorris M. and Allen, Richard V. *Learning to Read Through Experience*. New York: Appleton-Century-Crofts, 1963.

57. Leonard, George B. *Education and Ecstasy*. New York: Dell Publishing Co., Inc., 1968.

58. Lessinger, Leon, "The Principal and Accountability." *The Education Digest 37* (February 1972): 8–10.

59. Lindgren, Henry Clay. *Educational Psychology in the Classroom*. New York: John Wiley & Sons, Inc., 1972.

60. Lowen, Alexander. *The Language of the Body*. New York: Collier Books, 1958.
61. Lozanov, Georgii. "Foundations of Suggestology." Paper presented at the First International Conference on Suggestology, Sofia, Bulgaria, June, 1971.
62. Lozanov, Georgii. *Suggestology*. Sofia, Bulgaria: Izdatelsvo Navka; Iskustvo, 1971.
63. Lozanov, G. "Suggestopaedy in Primary Schools." *Suggestology and Suggestopaedia* 1 (January 1975): 1–13.
64. Lozanov, Georgii. "Excerpts from Foundations of Suggestology." Report presented at the International Symposium on Suggestology, Arlington, Virginia, May 10, 1975.
65. Maccoby, Eleanor Emmons, and Jacklin, Carol Nagy. "Myth, Reality and Shades of Gray: What We Know and Don't Know About Sex Differences." *Human Development in Today's World*. Edited by Sheldon White. Boston: Educational Associates, 1976.
66. Maltz, M. *Psychocybernetics*. New York: Prentice-Hall, Inc., 1960.
67. Maslow, A. H. *Motivation and Personality*. New York: Harper & Row, Publishers, 1954.
68. Montessori, Maria. *Dr. Montessori's Own Handbook*. New York: Schocken Books, 1965.
69. Moustakas, Clark E. *The Authentic Teacher: Sensitivity and Awareness in the Classroom*. Cambridge, Mass.: Howard A. Doyle Publishing Co., 1966.
70. Nelson, Wally. "Experimentation with the Lozanov Method in Teaching Word Retention to Children with Learning Disabilities." *The Journal of Suggestive-Accelerative Learning and Teaching* 4 (Winter 1979) 228–271.
71. Nidich, S.; Seeman, W.; and Dreskin, T. "The Influence of Transcendental Meditation: A Replication." *Journal of Counseling Psychology* 20 (June 1973): 565–566.
72. Nystrand, Raphael O., and Cunningham, Luvern L. "Organizing Schools to Develop Human Capabilities." *To Nurture Humaneness: Commitment for the 70's*. Edited by Mary Margaret Scobey. Washington, D.C.: Association for Supervision and Curriculum Development, 1970.
73. Ostrander, Sheila, and Schroeder, Lynn. *Psychic Discoveries Behind the Iron Curtain*. New York: Bantam Books, 1973.
74. Ottina, J. R. *U.S. Office of Education Briefing Paper*. Washington, D.C.: Government Printing Office, 1974.
75. Petrie, Sidney and Stone, Robert B. *Hypno-cybernetics: Helping Yourself to a Rich New Life*. New York: Prentice-Hall, Inc., 1973.
76. Pettinger, Robert E., ed. *The First Five Minutes*. New York: Paul Martineau, 1960.
77. Petty, Walter T.; Petty, Dorothy C.; and Becking, Marjorie F. *Experiences in Language: Tools and Techniques for Language Arts Methods*. Boston: Allyn & Bacon, Inc., 1973.
78. Philipov, E. R. "Suggestology: The Use of Suggestion in Learning and Hypermnesia." Unpublished dissertation, U.S. International University, 1975.
79. Prichard, Allyn and Taylor, Jean. *Accelerating Learning: Use of Suggestion in*

the Classroom. Novato, Calif.: Academic Therapy Publications, 1980.
80. Purkey, William W. *Self-Concept and School Achievement*. Englewood Cliffs, N.J.: Prentice-Hall, Inc., 1970.
81. Racle, G. "A Suggestopaedic Experiment in Canada." *Suggestology and Suggestopaedia 1* (January 1975): 45–51.
82. Racle, Gabriel. "Application of Suggestology in French Language Learning Programs for Bi-lingual Training of Government Employees." Report presented at the International Symposium on Suggestology. Arlington, Virginia, May 10, 1975.
83. Roethlisberger, F. J., and Dickson, W. J. *Management and the Worker*. Cambridge, Mass.: Harvard University Press, 1939.
84. Rosenberg, Marshall B. *Diagnostic Teaching*. Seattle: Special Children Publications, 1968.
85. Rosenthal, Robert, and Jacobson, Lenore. *Pygmalion in the Classroom*. New York: Holt, Rinehart & Winston, 1968.
86. Rupley, William H. and Blair, Timothy R. *Reading Diagnosis and Remediation — A Primer for Classroom and Clinic*. Chicago: Rand McNally College Publishing Co., 1979.
87. Scheicher, Carl. "Rehabilitation With A Future Orientation." *Journal of Rehabilitation 41* (March–April, 1975): 12–18.
88. Schuster, D. H. "The Effects of Relaxation Exercises and Suggestions on the Learning of Spanish Words." Unpublished manuscript, Iowa State University, 1972.
89. Schuster, D. H. "The Effects of the Alpha Mental State, Indirect Suggestion and Associative Mental Activity on Learning Rare English Words." Unpublished manuscript, Iowa State University, 1973.
90. Schuster, D. H. "Relaxation While Taking A Test." Unpublished manuscript, Iowa State University, 1973.
91. Schulter, D. H., and Hasbrook, Richard. "A Comprehensive Evaluation of the Lozanov Method for the Improvement of Achievement and Attitudes in Classroom Learning." Iowa State University: Proposal to Educational Research and Development Program. Exxon Education Foundation, New York, June 16, 1975.
92. Schuster, D. H. "A Preliminary Evaluation of the Suggestive-Accelerative Lozanov Method in Teaching Beginning Spanish." *The Journal of Suggestive-Accelerative Learning and Teaching 1* (Spring 1976): 41–47.
93. Schuster, D. H.; Bordon, Ray Benitez; and Gritton, Charles A. *Suggestive-Accelerative Learning and Teaching: A Manual of Classroom Procedures Based on the Lozanov Method*. Des Moines, Iowa: Society for Suggestive-Accelerative Learning and Teaching, 1976.
94. Shostrom, Everett L. "An Inventory for the Measurement of Self-Actualization." *Educational and Psychological Measurement 24* (Summer 1964): 207–217.
95. Siks, Geraldine Brain. *Creative Dramatics*. New York: Harper & Row Publishers, 1958.
96. Silberman, Charles E. *Crisis in the Classroom*. New York: Random House, Inc., 1970.

97. Smirnova, N. L. "Progress in Experimental Instruction in the Course of Suggestology at the 'V. I. Lenin' Moscow State Pedagogical Institute." *Suggestology and Suggestopaedia 1* (March 1975): 14–23.

98. Smith, Frank. *Understanding Reading—A Psycholinquistic Analysis of Reading and Learning to Read.* New York: Holt, Rinehart & Winston, 1978.

99. Spache, George D., and Spache, Evelyn B. *Reading in the Elementary School.* Boston: Allyn & Bacon, Inc., 1973.

100. Strang, Ruth. *Reading Diagnosis and Remediation.* Newark, Delaware: I.R.A., 1968.

101. Strickland, Ruth G. *The Language Arts in the Elementary School.* Lexington, Mass.: D.L. Heath and Company, 1969.

102. Sullivan, H. S. *Concept of Modern Psychiatry.* Washington, D.C.: William Alanson Whitle Psychiatric Foundation, 1947.

103. Tashev, Todor, and Natan, Tanya. "Suggestion to Aid Teachers and Doctors." *Bulgaria Today 9* (1966):

104. *The Washington Post.* "A Classroom Breakthrough." March 21, 1974.

105. Tiedt, Sidney W., ed. *Teaching the Disadvantaged Child.* New York: Oxford University Press, 1968.

106. Torrance, E. Paul *Rewarding Creative Behavior.* Englewood Cliffs, N.J.: Prentice-Hall, 1965.

107. Trauger, Wilmer K. *Language Arts in the Elementary School.* New York: McGraw-Hill Book Company, 1963.

108. Troike-Saville, Muriel. *Foundations for Teaching English as a Second Language.* Englewood Cliffs: Prentice-Hall, Inc., 1976.

109. Usher, Richard, and Hanke, John. "The Third Force in Psychology and College Teacher Effectiveness Research at the University of Northern Colorado." *Colorado Journal of Educational Research 10* (1971): 2–10.

110. Wolkowski, Zbigniew William. "Suggestology: A Major Contribution by Bulgarian Scientists." Paper presented at the International Symposium on Suggestology, Arlington, Virginia, May 9, 1975.

111. Yotsukura, Sayo. "Suggestology and Language Teaching." Unpublished manuscript, Global University, 1975.

INDEX

175

DATE DUE

OCT 13 1988			
GAYLORD			PRINTED IN U.S.A.